THE MIND OF POE AND
OTHER STUDIES

THE MIND OF POE AND OTHER STUDIES

BY

KILLIS CAMPBELL

NEW YORK / RUSSELL & RUSSELL

PREFACE

THESE papers, with a single exception, were originally conceived without any thought of their being ultimately combined into a volume; but they have this in common, that they all deal with some matter that has been in dispute among students of Poe.

Of the seven papers that make up the volume, four have been published before, either in whole or in part. The papers on "Contemporary Opinion of Poe," "The Poe-Griswold Controversy," and "The Poe Canon" originally appeared in the *Publications of the Modern Language Association of America*, and are here reproduced, revised, and enlarged in each instance, with the permission of the Secretary of the Association, Professor Carleton Brown. The essay on "The Backgrounds of Poe" was originally published in part, under the title "Poe in Relation to his Times," in *Studies in Philology*, and is here reproduced with the permission of the editor, Professor George R. Coffman.

For aid in the reading of proofs I am deeply indebted to Professor Morgan Callaway, Jr., of the University of Texas, and to Professor Hyder E. Rollins, of Harvard University.

K. C.

AUSTIN, TEXAS
August 31, 1932

CONTENTS

The Mind of Poe 3

Contemporary Opinion of Poe 34

The Poe-Griswold Controversy 63

The Backgrounds of Poe 99

Self-revelation in Poe's Poems and Tales . 126

The Origins of Poe 147

The Poe Canon 187

THE MIND OF POE AND
OTHER STUDIES

THE MIND OF POE

I

THE poet Lanier is said to have remarked on one occasion, "The trouble with Poe was, he did not *know* enough." [1] To which Mr. J. M. Robertson, the well-known student and critic, retorts: "Alas, that is the trouble with all of us!" [2]

Just what Lanier meant by saying that Poe "did not know enough" I cannot feel sure. A very astute friend of mine suggests that he meant merely that Poe was a man of limited emotional experience and narrow sympathies. And if that be the case, Lanier was undoubtedly right. For although Poe had, as I shall presently endeavor to show, larger sympathies and wider human interests than is commonly allowed, it is not to be denied that his emotional sympathies were limited and his knowledge of life in some measure restricted. But I cannot bring myself to believe that this was what Lanier meant.

It is possible, I think, that Lanier meant merely that Poe had not read enough, that he did not know

[1] See *The Poems of Sidney Lanier*, edited by his wife, New York, 1884, pp. xxxv–xxxvi.

[2] J. M. Robertson, *New Essays Towards a Critical Method*, London, 1897, p. 106.

[3]

enough about books. And on that supposition, too, he was doubtless right. Poe had, to be sure, a pretty wide acquaintance with the literature of his own time.[1] He was familiar with Byron and Shelley and Moore, with Coleridge and Keats and Wordsworth, with Lowell and Longfellow, with Scott and Dickens and Disraeli, with Irving and Hawthorne and Simms, with De Quincey and Lamb and Hazlitt. He was not unfamiliar, moreover, with the chief writers of the age immediately preceding his own, with Gray and Cowper and Sterne and Walpole and Charles Brockden Brown. And he knew his Shakespeare, his Milton, and his Pope: he quotes from *Hamlet*, for instance, some thirty-eight times; from *Paradise Lost* as many as sixteen times; and from Pope no less than twenty-six times. But he had little or no first-hand knowledge of Chaucer or of Spenser; he had small acquaintance with Shakespeare's contemporaries, or with Milton's, or with Dryden's; and even among his own contemporaries there were some who appear to have been all but strangers to him — as Robert Browning and Thackeray and Jane Austen. Besides, his acquaintance with foreign literature seems to have been meagre and uncertain at best, being based largely on his work at college; while a great deal of his reading was professional, and hence was more or less perfunctory.

[1] In an article published in the University of Texas *Studies in English*, No. 5, pp. 166–196 (1925), I have endeavored to collect such evidence as we have as to the extent and nature of Poe's reading. See, also, for additional notes, *ibid.*, No. 7, pp. 175–180 (1927).

II

But it seems to me much more likely that Lanier had reference, not to Poe's reading, nor to any narrowness of sympathies and interests, but, rather, to the content of his mind, — in a word, to the extent of his knowledge, — and possibly also to the fibre of his mind. At least, it would seem only fair to take him at his word, — that "the trouble with Poe was, he did not know enough."

Wherein, then, let us ask, was Poe's intellectual stock-in-trade such as to exclude him from the company of those who might aspire to greatness? I have already touched on his knowledge of literature. What of his knowledge of language and the languages, of music and painting and sculpture, of history and philosophy and religion, of mathematics and astronomy, of physics and chemistry and botany and zoölogy, of the world of nature, of the political, industrial, and social life of his time, and of human life and experience in their more intimate and vital aspects? And wherein, if at all, were Poe's natural endowments such as to forbid his achieving eminence as a writer?

With respect to Poe's knowledge of his own language, the evidence at hand is not very satisfactory. There is nothing to show that he ever received any formal instruction in the subject, unless a statement to the effect that instruction would be given in "the English Language in its Anglo-Saxon form," made in

an announcement of courses for the University of
Virginia for 1825 and again for 1827 (that is, both
for the year preceding and for the year following
Poe's one session at the University), be construed as
pointing in that direction.[1] But it may be taken for
granted that as a boy he had the old-time drill in the
rudiments of English in the schools that he attended
in Richmond and London; and he inevitably acquired a good deal of incidental knowledge of grammatical forms and relations in his courses in the foreign languages, particularly in Latin. In his critical
papers, it may be added, he not infrequently draws
attention to some carelessness in grammatical construction; and he occasionally remarks on the history
of some word or ventures to suggest some etymology
of his own.[2]

Of the foreign languages he knew best Latin and
French. He had already begun the study of Latin in

[1] See *Enactments by the Rector and Visitors of the University of Virginia*, Charlottesville, 1825, p. 3; *ibid.*, revised edition, 1827, p. 17.
The West Point cadet in the thirties was, it seems, required to ac-
quaint himself in his second year with the elements of English grammar,
the instruction being given in connection with the courses in French
(see the *Annual Report of the Superintendent of the United States Military
Academy*, Washington, 1896, p. 135); but I can find nothing in the records
to indicate that any instruction in English grammar was given to the
first-year cadet at that time. Poe casually mentions Lindley Murray
twice in his collected writings (*The Complete Works of Edgar Allan Poe*,
ed. Harrison, New York, 1902, xiv, 181, 212: hereafter referred to as
"*Poe's Works*"); and once he mentions the bulky grammar of Goold
Brown (*ibid.*, p, 212); and once, also, he makes merry in exposing the
inadequacies of a contemporary grammatical treatise, Pue's *English
Grammar* (*ibid.*, x, 167 f.).
[2] See, for instance, *Poe's Works*, ii, 28; iv, 205, 290; vi, 132; xiv, 45,
69, 223.

[6]

1818, when but nine years old; for in that year his foster-father, John Allan, wrote his business partner in Richmond that Edgar could read Latin "pretty sharply."[1] And he continued the study of Latin at the academy in Richmond (where he won local distinction for his facility in "capping verses" from Horace) and throughout his year at the University of Virginia, where he was listed at the end of the session among those who "excelled" in the subject.[2] His Latin quotations, it must be admitted, are sometimes inaccurate, — that is, verbally inaccurate (he is very rarely inaccurate, so far as I have observed, in his spelling of the Latin,[3] and this in spite of the fact that he was a notoriously bad speller).[4] Of fifteen quotations from Horace, for instance, four are inexact; and of sixteen from Virgil that I have noted, five are inexact. But about the same ratio holds for his quotations from Pope, whom he quotes inaccu-

[1] The *Sewanee Review*, xx, 206 (April, 1912).

[2] *Poe's Works*, i, 61.

[3] I have noted the spelling *agressi* (*Poe's Works*, iv, 236), and the substitution of *dicite* for *discite* (*ibid.*, xvi, 6). But the reader must be on his guard against assuming that Poe's citations from the foreign languages as reproduced in the various editions of his works represent precisely what he wrote; in most cases the editors have silently corrected the errors which appear in the original texts. In some cases, too, it is but fair to Poe to say, the error may be due to the printer's carelessness, as must surely have been the case, for instance, with two inaccuracies in the spelling of the Latin noted by Harrison in the text of "Loss of Breath" (*Poe's Works*, ii, 366).

[4] There are, for example, in the score of letters brought together in the "Valentine Letters" (*Edgar Allan Poe Letters . . . in the Valentine Museum, Richmond, Virginia*, ed. Mary Newton Stanard, Philadelphia, 1925) some ten or a dozen slips in spelling.

[7]

rately eight times in a total of twenty-six passages cited. And of some ninety quotations from the Bible, more than half are inexact.[1] Evidently he was accustomed to quote from memory. It is plain, too, that he did not scruple to twist or garble a quotation when he felt that this would serve his purpose.

It is much the same with his knowledge of French. He probably began the study of French while at school in London, and he was graduated in the subject after one year at the University of Virginia, being (as in Latin) among the starred graduates.[2] At West Point in 1830 he ranked third in French in a class of eighty-seven. Among the books that he drew out of the library of the University of Virginia in 1826 were three works in French, — Voltaire's *Histoire Particulière* and Rollin's *Histoire Ancienne* and *Histoire Romaine*,[3] — from which it may be inferred that he had already, at the age of seventeen, acquired the habit of reading extra-curricular French works in the original. His quotations from the French, which abound, even to excess, throughout his writings, are usually accurate in form, his chief lapses in this regard being in certain twisted accents and false genders; but in idiom he was not infrequently at fault, as Miss Edith Philips has shown.[4]

[1] See W. M. Forrest, *Biblical Allusions in Poe*, New York, 1928, pp. 152 f., and see also *Studies in Philology*, xxvii, 548 (July, 1930).

[2] James A. Harrison, *The Life of Edgar Allan Poe*, New York, 1902, p. 61.

[3] J. H. Ingram, *Life and Letters of Poe*, London, 1880, pp. 42–43.

[4] "The French of Edgar Allan Poe," *American Speech*, ii, 270–274 (March, 1927).

Of his knowledge of German and Spanish and Italian I do not feel so certain. That he could make shift to read brief passages of easy German has, I think, been established,[1] but just how far his acquaintance with the language extended is not clear. In every likelihood, his first-hand acquaintance with German was small. There is no record of his having had any instruction in the subject,[2] and he quotes from the German not above two dozen times,— once for as many as ten lines from Humboldt, and again for half a dozen lines from Novalis,[3] — but in each instance, as Professor Schreiber has shown, he relies on another for the translation that he gives.[4] He writes (with reference to a book) that "er lasst sich nicht lesen," [5] he twice speaks of Werther's *Lieden*

A friend of mine, a Romance scholar, to whom I once submitted some specimens of Poe's French, remarked that it was "pretty rocky"; and Miss Philips (p. 273) characterizes his French as "curious" at times, especially in its idiom, and she points out (p. 270) that Baudelaire, in translating his stories, altered his French in numerous instances. Nevertheless, it is quite clear that Poe had a ready reading knowledge of French.

As to Poe's fondness for interlarding his essays and tales with French and other foreign phrases and quotations, see below, p. 31.

[1] See Gustav Gruener, "Poe's Knowledge of German," *Modern Philology*, II, 125 f. (June, 1904). But see also Carl Schreiber, "Mr. Poe at his Conjurations Again," the *Colophon*, II, 1–11 (May, 1930). Professor Schreiber gives it as his opinion that Poe "never read more than three pages of consecutive German prose, if indeed he read that number."

[2] Except in so far as this is implied in a statement in the *Enactments by the Rector and Visitors of the University of Virginia*, both of 1825 and of 1827 (pp. 3 and 17, respectively), that German "shall be taught" in the School of Modern Languages.

[3] *Poe's Works*, v, 1 f.; XVI, 299.

[4] The *Colophon*, II, 5 f.

[5] *Poe's Works*, IV, 134.

[9]

(*sic*),[1] and in the printed texts he consistently omits his umlauts.[2] Spanish and Italian and Greek were among his subjects at the University of Virginia, and it is tolerably certain that he could make some headway in the translation of each. He must have been least at home with Spanish, in view of the fact that his quotations from the Spanish (seven in all by my reckoning) exhibit minor inaccuracies in quite half the lines cited. His quotations from Italian and Greek, on the other hand, are with few exceptions accurate, — though he confuses a "xi" with a "zeta" in one case [3] and with a "sigma" in another,[4] and he adopts the wrong gender form with one of his Greek relatives.[5] He translates quite correctly, however, in a note on one of his stories, a passage of twenty lines from Plato's *Republic*; [6] and tradition has it that he attracted attention to himself on one occasion while at the University of Virginia by turning a passage from Tasso into English verse as a class exercise.[7] It

---

[1] *Poe's Works*, VI, 249; the *Democratic Review*, XIX, 32 (July, 1846).

[2] This blunder may, however, be due to the printer, most American printing establishments of the time probably being without the necessary type; and in at least one piece of writing in his autograph, — that of a scrap of manuscript preserved at the Fordham Cottage, in which he comments on Coleridge's borrowing of two lines from Schiller (for his "Ovidian Elegiac Metre"), — Poe enters the umlaut quite legibly in one instance, in the use of the word *flüssige* (though it must be added that in the same passage he omits the umlaut with the words *füllt* and *Säule*).

[3] *Poe's Works*, XIV, 70.

[4] *Ibid.*, II, 117 (text of the *Broadway Journal*).   [5] *Ibid.*, IV, 134.

[6] *Ibid.*, p. 204; and in his *Politian* he quotes a poetic rendering of a famous passage from the *Odyssey*, perhaps translated by himself (see T. O. Mabbott's edition of *Politian*, Richmond, 1923, p. 64).

[7] Ingram, p. 41.

appears that he also had some slight knowledge of Hebrew, which was among the subjects required by the "Rector and Visitors" of the University of Virginia in the School of Ancient Languages,[1] though this must have been exceedingly slight.

Of his knowledge of the fine arts — of music, and painting, and sculpture, the theatre and dancing — I am likewise uncertain, though it was, we may assume, neither wide nor deep. For at least one year in London he had lessons in dancing.[2] He sang well, so it has been held; [3] and he is likewise said to have played the flute; [4] and we know that he was fond of the piano and of instrumental music generally. In an early letter (written in 1835) he remarks that he has been making "some odd chromatic experiments" by way of testing the music of some of his own lines; [5] and elsewhere he reveals an acquaintance with technical terms in music.[6] In certain of his essays, especially those written about 1845, he comments on the opera and on theatrical performances in New York City, which he attended from time to time.[7] He was personally acquainted with Murdock, Junius Brutus Booth, and Mrs. Mowatt; and he inherited from his

[1] See for a brief discussion of his knowledge of Hebrew, Forrest's *Biblical Allusions in Poe*, pp. 205 f.; and note that the word *huggab* used by Poe in "A Tale of Jerusalem" (*Poe's Works*, II, 219) does not appear in any English translation of the Scriptures, but apparently represents Poe's anglicizing of the original Hebrew.

[2] The "Valentine Letters," p. 319.

[3] Hervey Allen, *Israfel*, p. 144.

[4] *Ibid.*, pp. 43, 144.

[5] The *Century Magazine*, CVII, 654 (March, 1924).

[6] *Poe's Works*, X, 197; XVI, 8.   [7] *Ibid.*, XII, 184 f.

parents an interest in the actor's art, although he took no part in theatrical performances, so far as we know, after his youthful years in Richmond.

Some acquaintance with painting is indicated by sundry comments here and there on the work of the world's great artists, including Michael Angelo, Leonardo, Raphael, Titian, Correggio, Rubens, and Poussin. He was personally acquainted with the portrait painter S. S. Osgood and with R. M. Sully (nephew of the famous Philadelphian), to each of whom he sat for a portrait.[1] In two uncollected articles in the *Broadway Journal*, he essays to pass judgment on the authenticity of an alleged Titian's "Venus,"[2] and it appears that he wrote still other art-criticisms for the *Broadway Journal*. He exhibits also in various passages an interest (though doubtless superficial) in sculpture and in household decoration. He wrote an article of a dozen pages on the subject of landscape gardening;[3] and published a signed article in 1845 on "The Ivory Christ."[4]

Such knowledge of history as he possessed he perhaps came into largely at haphazard. He probably had in his boyhood some instruction in general his-

[1] He had, it seems, some gift for drawing: see Hervey Allen, p. 145; Mrs. Weiss, *The Home Life of Poe*, New York, 1907, p. 122; and an article in *Time* for October 6, 1930, p. 56, touching three pencil portraits — of himself, his wife, and his early sweetheart, Sarah Elmira Royster — said to have been made by himself.

[2] Margaret Alterton, *Origins of Poe's Critical Theory*, Iowa City, 1925, p. 85.

[3] *Poe's Works*, IV, 259 f.

[4] Margaret Alterton, *op. cit.*, p. 84.

tory; we know from one of the bills submitted to his foster-father for his schooling in London that he received there some instruction in English history; [1] and he drew from the library while at the University of Virginia several treatises on American and European history.[2] Apparently, though, he had not read widely in the work of the great historians, Gibbon and Niebuhr and Bancroft being the only modern historians of note with whom he reveals any familiarity. On the other hand, the evidence is overwhelming that he kept well abreast of the history of his own times, and he was peculiarly fascinated by contemporary accounts of voyages of exploration and discovery.[3]

Poe early developed an interest in philosophy. In common with the more acute minds of New England in his day, he was genuinely attracted to German philosophical thinking. He knew something of Kant and Hegel and Fichte and Leibnitz. Apparently he drew the idea underlying his story of "Morella" from Schelling's theorizing on the subject of identity, to which he indirectly credits it.[4] He quotes from both Aristotle and Plato; and he alludes both in his

[1] The *Dial*, LX, 144 (February 17, 1916).

[2] *Poe's Works*, I, 47.

[3] See, for instance, his article (as yet uncollected) on Reynolds's "Exploring Expedition" (*Graham's Magazine*, XXIII, 164 f. [September, 1843]), and his review of Reynolds's report on his earlier expedition into the South Seas (*Poe's Works*, IX, 306). He reveals also a familiarity (see below, p. 168) with various other accounts of exploring expeditions, including those of Lewis and Clark, Captain Cook, and Benjamin Morrell.

[4] *Poe's Works*, II, 29.

prose and in his verse to Plato's doctrine of ideas.[1]
He cites passages also from Comte and Pascal. Of
the English philosophers he appears to have known
best Locke and Mill and Bentham. In his "Morella"
he cites Locke's definition of "personal identity" as
consisting in the "sameness of a rational being";[2]
and he ridiculed in various places the doctrines of
Mill and Bentham. But how accurate or how profound his knowledge of philosophy was, I hesitate to
say: it is a field in which further investigations must
be made before we can be sure of our ground. I
hazard the guess, however, that Poe had little exact
or systematic knowledge of the subject, — though it
is plain that he had, somehow, picked up a good many
scraps of philosophical information, which he used to
advantage in both his stories and his essays, and
especially in his early tales and his pseudo-meta-
physical treatise *Eureka*, and that he superposed
upon these bits of philosophical lore a good many
metaphysical notions of his own, some of them quite
seriously meant, and others dictated by his predilec-
tion for mystification and hoaxing.[3]

Religion and religious thought, on the other hand,

[1] Once, to be sure, in an essay ascribed to him by his editors (*Poe's Works*, XII, 164), he speaks disparagingly of Plato; but if this essay be actually the work of Poe, it may reasonably be assumed that he wrote in a wilful and wayward mood.

[2] *Poe's Works*, II, 29.

[3] Poe almost invariably spoke disapprovingly of the Transcendentalists, it may be noted, but, for all that, he possessed something in common
with them. He asserts, for example, in his *Eureka* (*Poe's Works*, XVI, 10)
that "the Universe is a Plot of God," — with which may be compared

[14]

seem to have interested Poe but little, save on the
more abstract side. As a child he was drilled in the
Episcopal catechism; [1] he knew something of the history of the Episcopal Church; [2] and it is probable
that he was acquainted with the tenets both of the
Episcopal Church and of the Presbyterian, — though
I am persuaded that he cared not the least for matters
of dogma. At the same time, he appears to have been
deeply interested in such profounder ideas as the
meaning and nature of the Deity. The origin of the
universe and God's relation to the universe form the
central ideas of his *Eureka*; and he speculates on
similar ideas in the introduction to his "Mesmeric
Revelation" and in "The Power of Words." The
same speculative tendency in religious matters reveals itself also in his early poem "Al Aaraaf," in
which he develops the idea that God reveals himself
not alone in knowledge and in power but also in
beauty. By one of his critics he has been held to have
been "a soured and self-willed unbeliever"; [3] but
this view is contradicted in a dozen passages in his

Emerson's statement in the "American Scholar" that nature is the "web
of God." Elsewhere he gives his endorsement to the ancient doctrine of
the "flux" of things, asserting at one point (*ibid.*, x, 160 n.) — again
quite in the manner of Emerson — that "all things are in a perpetual
state of progress; that nothing in nature is *perfected*." And in one of the
earliest of his stories he quotes (with implied approval) the statement of
Godwin in his *Mandeville* that "invisible things are the only realities"
(*ibid.*, II, 154).

[1] The *Dial*, LX, 144 (February 17, 1916).

[2] *Poe's Works*, VIII, 239 f.; IX, 33 f.

[3] A. H. Strong, *The American Poets and their Theology*, Philadelphia,
1916, p. 161.

writings. In at least two of his essays, he avows a belief in the immortality of the soul; [1] in one of his early essays he subscribes without qualification to the doctrine of the "infallibility of the Divine word"; [2] in another he speaks of God's omnipotence and omniscience; [3] and in a brief critical notice, apparently from his pen, in the *Broadway Journal* [4] he boldly declares that "men deny a God only with their lips."

In mathematics, a subject that always attracted him, Poe's standing at West Point was seventeenth in a class of eighty-seven; and he not infrequently employs mathematical terms or formulas in his stories. In his notes on *Eureka*, furthermore, he enters upon a number of mathematical-astronomical speculations in support of the theories there advanced, which, however inaccurate or immature they may be, evince at least a mathematical turn and considerable ingenuity in the manipulation of figures, and would seem to indicate an acquaintance with the subject well beyond that possessed by the average layman of intelligence at the present time. [5]

He also had acquired a good deal of information, superficial though it may have been, about astron-

[1] *Poe's Works*, x, 159; xiv, 273.

[2] *Ibid.*, x, 6, 159.

[3] *Ibid.*, xvi, 254. And see also a brief note on the "Study of Nature" (*Burton's Gentleman's Magazine*, vi, 235 [May, 1840]), in the course of which he speaks of "the infinite power, wisdom and goodness of the Great Cause of all being."

[4] ii, 388 (December 27, 1845).

[5] See in this connection A. R. Wallace, *Edgar Allan Poe*, New York [1930], pp. 5, 8.

omy. His interest in the subject probably had its origin in the circumstance that his foster-father owned
a telescope, which stood on the porch of his spacious
home in Richmond,[1] and through which the boy Poe
must often have gazed at the stars. He made use of
a number of astronomical terms in one of his earliest
tales, "Hans Pfaall"; he brings into play his knowledge of astronomy in still other tales [2] and in several
of his poems, including "Al Aaraaf" and "Ulalume";
and he resorts to extensive astronomical speculations
in his *Eureka*, where he discourses upon such topics
as the speed of the stars, the diameters of certain
planets, the weight of the earth, the distances of the
planets from one another, and the circle described by
"Leverrier's planet" (the recently discovered Neptune).[3] In his "Ulalume" he avails himself of the
information, with which, I imagine, not every layman is acquainted, that Venus as seen through the
telescope assumes in some positions the aspect of a
crescent.[4]

In connection with his study of astronomy he had
also picked up considerable information about physics and the mechanical arts. He touches in various

[1] Woodberry, *Edgar Allan Poe*, Boston, 1885, p. 25.

[2] *Poe's Works*, ii, 61, 62 f.; iv, 4; v, 248, 253; vi, 140, 209 f.

[3] *Ibid.*, xvi, 340 f., 348, 252, 283, 279 f., 284. From his notes on
Eureka (see especially p. 330), it is plain that he endeavored to keep
abreast of the discoveries in astronomical science.

[4] See also Quinn, Baugh, and Howe, *The Literature of America*, p. 24
(of the notes), for his alertness in fixing the time of the poem early on an
October morning when both Venus and the moon would be crescent and
"would be in conjunction with the constellation of Leo."

places on the law of gravitation, and he adopted and applied this principle in *Eureka* in his theorizing as to the origins of the universe, and he employed it for imaginative purposes in his "Hans Pfaall." Another of his stories, "A Descent into the Maelström," is based on a pseudo-physical principle which he attributes to Archimedes;[1] namely, that "a cylinder, swimming in a vortex, "offers more resistance to its suction, and [is] drawn in with greater difficulty than an equally bulky body, of any form whatever." And in half a dozen tales he utilizes information that he had collected about aeronautics. He suggests, in an article written early in the forties,[2] the feasibility of crossing the Atlantic in an air-ship. In one of his early stories he represents a balloon as passing above the North Pole,[3] and in another story he discourses about the speed of air-ships and about transcontinental air-routes.[4] Elsewhere he speaks of the physics of music,[5] of the "orange ray of the spectrum,"[6] of polarized rays,[7] of the galvanic battery and its possible use,[8] and of the mechanism of telegraphy and of electrotyping.[9]

He knew something, too, about chemistry, though so far as I can learn he at no time had any set instruction in the subject. He had somewhere learned, for instance, that bichloride of mercury is a wood

---

[1] See *Modern Language Notes*, XLII, 520 (December, 1927).
[2] *Burton's Gentleman's Magazine*, VI, 247 (May, 1840).
[3] *Poe's Works*, II, 88.   [4] *Ibid.*, VI, 206.
[5] *Ibid.*, XVI, 8.   [6] *Ibid.*, pp. 17 f.
[7] *Ibid.*, II, 5.   [8] *Ibid.*, V, 173, 261.   [9] *Ibid.*, VI, 98 f.

preservative, and he used this information to bolster up his climax in "The Gold-Bug"; and in "The Thousand-and-Second Tale of Scheherazade" he describes a process by which ice may be manufactured chemically.[1] His story "Eiros and Charmion" turns upon a situation in which all nitrogen is extracted from the air by reason of the approach of a comet, with the result that the earth is consumed by fire.

He had likewise garnered a number of learned facts about botany and geology, as seen in his employment of technical botanical terms in "Al Aaraaf" [2] and in several of the tales,[3] and in his mention of geological terms in his essay on Stonehenge and in one or another of his stories.[4] He had some knowledge, also, of biology, and indeed he collaborated in the translation and adaptation of a book on shells, his *Conchologist's First Book*.[5]

It has been held that he had considerable knowledge of the law.[6] He registered as a student of law in Philadelphia in 1843;[7] but such legal study as he undertook he can scarcely have carried very far. Moreover, the only substantial evidence of his acquaintance with law is furnished by his use here and

[1] *Ibid.*, p. 99.   [2] *Ibid.*, VII, 25, 26.
[3] See especially "The Thousand-and-Second Tale of Scheherazade," *ibid.*, VI, 92–93.
[4] *Ibid.*, XIV, 112; II, 40; III, 231.
[5] He may also have had some hand in a treatise on natural history; see his review of *A Synopsis of Natural History*, ostensibly the work of Thomas Wyatt, in *Burton's Gentleman's Magazine*, V, 61 (July, 1839).
[6] Margaret Alterton, *Origins of Poe's Critical Theory*, pp. 46 f.
[7] Hervey Allen, *Israfel*, p. 565.

there of technical terms from that field (as "in fee
simple impartite," "ex parte," "non est inventus,"
etc.[1]) and by several reviews of legal reports.[2] But
his technical terms he may have gleaned from his
reading, or have drawn from works of reference; and
for his reviews of law treatises he may well have
called in the aid of specialists in that field.[3]

Poe's knowledge of nature is traditionally held to
have been slight.[4] The evidence afforded by his
poems obviously lends support to that view. Only
one of his lyrics, "Evening Star," deals with nature
as its central theme, and nature plays a noteworthy
subsidiary part in less than a dozen others. Even in
those, moreover, in which it plays some part, the
nature introduced may scarcely be said to be natural:
apparently it was drawn largely from books, as in the
case of his mention of the albatross in "Romance"
and of the nyctanthes and the "Nelumbo bud" in
"Al Aaraaf," or in his very happy mention, in "For
Annie," of the pansy and the rosemary.[5] So, too, in
his tales, while natural objects are often mentioned,

---

[1] *Poe's Works*, IV, 177; XII, 36.

[2] *Southern Literary Messenger*, II, 50 f. (December, 1835); *ibid.*,
pp. 731 f. (October, 1836).

[3] Similarly it might be argued from Poe's use of certain technical
terms from physiology and medicine (as *tunica albuginea, os sesamoideum
pollicis pedis*, and aneurism of the aorta [*Poe's Works*, VI, 121 f., 157])
that he had made a study of medicine; but surely no student of Poe
would seriously uphold such a supposition.

[4] See, for instance, Woodberry, *Edgar Allan Poe*, Boston, 1885,
p. 252; and H. M. Belden, *Observation and Imagination in Coleridge and
Poe: A Contrast* [Hartford, 1928], pp. 31 f.

[5] Evidently suggested by his reading of *Hamlet*.

it is pretty clear that he drew mainly on his reading. In his *Arthur Gordon Pym* he catalogues a number of birds (thirteen in one passage) belonging to the South Seas; and in the same story he enumerates sixteen varieties of fish from the South Seas, drawing in each instance, I suspect, on Benjamin Morrell's *Four Voyages*. Manifestly he relied on books also for his description of shells in his treatise on conchology.[1] His landscapes are as a rule of the fabric of his own fancy; and in some passages in which he would give the impression that he had drawn from life, it is reasonably certain that he was relying on books or on the testimony of others.[2] It may, then, be conceded that he rarely wrote "with his eye on the object."

But there are not wanting references to nature that must have been based on personal observation. Again and again Poe introduces into his writings glimpses of the sea, with which he beyond any doubt had an intimate and sympathetic acquaintance.[3] Once at

[1] *The Conchologist's First Book: or, a System of Testaceous Malacology,* Philadelphia, 1839.

[2] See, for instance, his description of a Louisiana landscape in "The Elk" (*Poe's Works*, v, 157 f.).

[3] See especially his *Arthur Gordon Pym*, "Hans Pfaall," "MS. Found in a Bottle," "The Descent into the Maelström," and "The Balloon Hoax"; and note certain very specific references to the sea, — as his mention of the "low, sullen murmurs of the sea" (*Poe's Works*, II, 358) and of a "moaning sound, not unlike the distant reverberation of surf" (*ibid.*, IV, 208) and of the bellowing of the sea in the earliest text of "Bon-Bon," and a brief passage in one of his "Omniana" (*Burton's Gentleman's Magazine*, VI, 236 [May, 1840]), in which he says of the ocean: "I wonder any being who affects *taste* would venture to assert that this immense body of water presents only sameness and monotony. To me it seems that even the colors and sounds are little less varied than those we see or hear in the midst of the most luxuriant landscape."

least he describes briefly but realistically a snowy evening,[1] and once a rainy, blustery evening.[2] At several points in his tales he makes occasion to speak of vegetables or garden plants, among those referred to being cabbages, cucumbers, turnips, onions, celery, cauliflower, Irish potatoes, corn, parsley, pumpkins, watermelons, milkweed, and purslain. He mentions, too, at one point or another, a variety of fruits, including blackberries, raspberries, gooseberries, grapes, figs, apricots, apples. Of trees he mentions, among others, the cypress, the cherry, the box, the ash, the cedar, the sycamore, the catalpa, the red bud, the palmetto, the magnolia, the poplar, the walnut, the maple, and the sassafras, all of which he apparently knew at first hand.[3] And while many of his birds and animals are drawn from books, others came as surely from personal observation.[4] A similar generalization

[1] *Poe's Works*, ii, 132.

[2] *Ibid.*, iv, 141 f.

[3] In "The Island of the Fay" (*ibid.*, p. 198) he writes accurately enough of the "white flakes of the bark of the sycamore"; and in "Landor's Cottage" (*ibid.*, vi, 258 f.) he gives an elaborate but realistic picture of a forest scene which he associates with the vicinity of New York City.

[4] In one of his stories (*Poe's Works*, v, 88) he speaks of the "pale blue eye" of the vulture; in another of eyes that "protruded from their sockets like those of the green dragon-fly" (*ibid.*, vi, 84); in another of a boat giving itself a shake "just as a dog does in coming out of the water" (*ibid.*, ii, 236); and in his "Poetic Principle" (*ibid.*, xiv, 270) he speaks of the "aromatic air of a Southern midsummer night." Among other realistic references to nature may be mentioned his characterization of a codfish as being "all head and shoulders" (*ibid.*, iv, 192), and his description of the yellow poplar or tulip tree in "The Gold-Bug" (*ibid.*, v, 109 f.) and again and even more vividly in "Landor's Cottage" (*ibid.*, vi, 260 f.).

máy be made with regard to his knowledge of flowers: from one or another of his stories it may reasonably be inferred that he had a sympathetic acquaintance with the rose, the lily-of-the-valley, the buttercup, the tulip, the pansy, the violet, the hyacinth, and the laurel. It is said that there grew by his door-step at Fordham a bed of "mignonette, heliotrope, and dahlias,"[1] in the cultivation of which he may be presumed to have had some part, and that outside the door of one of the homes in which he lived in Philadelphia there was in summer "a blaze of hollyhocks and geraniums."[2] During his last three years in the Allan home in Richmond, moreover, Poe lived in a spacious Southern mansion that looked out upon a garden in which a variety of vegetables and fruits grew in summer;[3] and it may be taken for granted that he sometimes visited the farm which Mr. Allan owned in Goochland County, near Richmond. There are, too, in his stories, passages in which I think I find evidence of a sympathy with animals, — with a dog in one instance and with a herd of buffaloes that meet an accidental death in another.[4] He owned at one time a pet bobolink,[5] and his letters reveal his loyalty to the family cat.[6] In one of his tales he writes, with evident sincerity, in praise of bypaths

[1] Woodberry, ii, 228.
[2] Hervey Allen, *Israfel*, p. 537. See also, in this connection, Miss Mary E. Phillips, *Poe — the Man*, Philadelphia, 1926, p. 1459.
[3] Allen, p. 127.
[4] *Poe's Works*, iii, 30; iv, 81; v, 144.
[5] Woodberry, ii, 216, 228.   [6] *Poe's Works*, xvii, 167.

as affording the proper point of view for the observation of a natural landscape.[1] We know that he was fond of swimming and of roaming in the woods; and it appears that he was fond of boating, of hunting, and of excursions into the country.[2]

It would seem, then, that although Poe's first-hand acquaintance with nature was comparatively slight, he had, for all that, a closer acquaintance with nature than is commonly assumed,[3] and it is plain that he was not without a genuine sympathy for nature in certain of its aspects.

What of Poe's knowledge of the political, industrial, and social life of his time? It has almost universally been held that he cared little for the life that went on about him. But, as I endeavor to show in a later essay,[4] this view is not sustained by an examination of his writings. His poems, it may be granted,

[1] *Poe's Works*, v, 158.

[2] Harrison, *Life of Poe*, p. 24.

[3] He rarely enters, to be sure, into an elaborate description of any natural object; but the same is true of Emerson (as Professor Foerster, *Nature in American Literature* [New York, 1923], p. 62, has observed) and also of Bryant. And he was partial to nature in its abstracter and more spiritual aspects, as is indicated in the following extraordinary passage from "The Island of the Fay" (*Poe's Works*, IV, 194): "I love, indeed, to regard the dark valleys, and the grey rocks, and the waters that silently smile, and the forests that sigh in uneasy slumbers, and the proud watchful mountains that look down upon all — I love to regard these as themselves but the colossal members of one vast animate and sentient whole — a whole whose form (that of the sphere) is the most perfect and most inclusive of all; whose path is among the associate planets; whose meek handmaiden is the moon; whose mediate sovereign is the sun; whose life is eternity; whose thought is that of God." And see also a very striking passage in "The Power of Words" (*ibid.*, VI, 140).

[4] See below, pp. 99 f.

throw little light on the matter; but his tales not only reveal a genuine interest in the political and economic life of his day, but they also reveal a genuine concern about the social life of his time; while his critical and miscellaneous papers everywhere testify to his interest in the multifarious social and industrial activities of his age.

In several of his early reviews he touches on slavery in the South.[1] In one of his papers he pleads for a more rational educational system in Virginia; in another he dwells on the duty of our nation to "remunerate scientific research" and to bear its part in contributing "to the aggregate of human knowledge"; in another he laments the lack of liberty of opinion in America; in still another he complains of the sensitiveness of Americans to criticism by foreigners and of their testiness of temper; in yet another he praises the Southerner's chivalry and attitude of deference to women, but in another he condemns the occasional spirit of barbarity displayed in rural sections of the South; in still others he voices his disapproval of the tendency to build up an "aristocracy of dollars" in America, of the contemporary craze for reforms, — of the "uplifters," "progress mongers," and "reform cranks" or "reform demigods"; of the "rush of the age," of the diffuseness of American legislative oratory, of the "popgunnery of the news-

[1] See, in particular, a notice of J. K. Paulding's *Slavery in the United States* (*Poe's Works*, VIII, 269 f.), and the uncollected notice of Ingraham's *The Southwest* (*Southern Literary Messenger*, II, 122 f. [December, 1835]), in which he gives very frankly his attitude toward slavery.

paper press," of the craze for "glitter" and "glare" in household decoration.

In a single story, "The Thousand-and-Second Tale of Scheherazade," — to cite also something of evidence from his more imaginative writings, — he evinces an interest in so wide a variety of subjects as the wonders of the Mammoth Cave of Kentucky, the miracle of steamboat navigation on the Hudson, a petrified forest in Texas, orchids, caterpillars and lion ants, a flock of pigeons two hundred and fifty miles long, the eccaleobion or incubator, the speed of a passenger train on the London and Northwestern Railway, the daguerreotype, and — by way of climaxing his story — the fashion of wearing bustles.[1]

It seems to me not improbable, moreover, that Poe had both a wider and a deeper knowledge of human life in its more personal and vital aspects than is commonly supposed. Living largely to himself, he was, I dare say, not a very sociable being, a man who made little display (save in his own home) of human sympathies; though he always had friends, he had few intimate friends; and he had never known the joys and sorrows of parenthood.[2] Barring a warmly felt sympathy for the Negro slave, he exhibited in his

---

[1] See also the series of papers contributed by Poe to the *Columbia Spy* in 1844, in which he gossips much in the manner of the newspaper "columnist" of to-day on matters of current interest in New York and Brooklyn at the time. These papers have recently been collected by J. E. Spannuth and T. O. Mabbott under the title *Doings of Gotham* (Pottsville, Pennsylvania, 1929).

[2] Such references as he makes to children, it may be noted, are not infrequently cynical in tone.

writings little knowledge of the laboring man and of the commonplace things of every-day existence. He served for a time as a soldier, but he never bore arms in defense of his country; he travelled little save in his youth; and he saw but little of social life after leaving the Allan home in 1827. On the other hand, he suffered as no other one of our major poets has suffered from poverty and adversity. Though he could hardly have had any recollection of his parents, the shadow of their poverty and of their wretchedness during their last years haunted him always. And though he enjoyed during his more impressionable years the comparative luxury of the Allan home, this only served to intensify his suffering when, after a display of waywardness and pique on his part, he was, in effect, driven from that home, disowned, and, as he felt, disgraced.[1] He served, at one time or another, as a common soldier; as a clerk, so it has been held;[2] and also as a day-laborer in a brick-yard,[3] if another story may be credited; he aspired, at different times, to be a teacher, a government clerk, a lawyer. He was so human as to find entertainment in secret writing, in crossword puzzles, and in riddles of all sorts, and he was interested throughout his life in athletic sports and exercises.

The human note in the man comes out clearly enough in his letters, and particularly in certain refer-

[1] See the "Valentine Letters," pp. 55 f.
[2] Miss Mary E. Phillips, *Poe — the Man*, p. 309.
[3] Mrs. Susan Archer Talley Weiss, *The Home Life of Poe*, p. 63.

ences to his wife and to his parents. He wrote Lowell in 1845 wishing him in his marriage "as substantial happiness" as he had derived from his own marriage.[1] In an early letter, to Beverly Tucker, he laments the fact that he has never known parental love.[2] And in one of his later essays he takes occasion to condemn the prejudice against the player's profession, remarking at the same time that he was "himself the son of an actress" and that "no earl was ever prouder of his earldom than he of the descent from a woman who, although well-born, hesitated not to consecrate to the drama her brief career of genius and of beauty."[3]

Limited, then, though his sympathies must have been in some directions, and restricted though his interests almost inevitably were, I am of the opinion that his sympathies and interests were a good deal wider than most of his biographers and critics have been inclined to admit. He had, if I read him aright, immense intellectual curiosity and an extraordinarily large stock of general information.

III

What, finally, of the fibre of Poe's mind, of his natural endowments, and of his intellectual integrity? No one, so far as I know, has ever denied to Poe the possession of a peculiarly acute and active mind. Mr. John Macy asserts, indeed, that he "met his in-

[1] Woodberry, II, 104.
[2] The *Century Magazine*, CVII, 654 (March, 1924).
[3] *Poe's Works*, XII, 186.

tellectual equal in the flesh" only once: when in 1845 he received a brief visit from Lowell.[1] That he had keen insight and superior powers of discrimination is indicated by the fact that virtually all of his important critical judgments have been sustained by time. That he had unusual gifts for generalization and for abstraction is made plain by his *Eureka* and by certain of his essays. And that he had extraordinary powers of analysis comes out everywhere, — in his critical reviews, in his studies in sensation, in his ratiocinative and pseudo-scientific stories, in his solving of ciphers and cryptographs. He had, moreover, as is abundantly evidenced in the construction of his stories especially, fine powers of synthesis. And no American author, I think, has exhibited more of clarity in his writing, none more of independence in his thinking, and few, if any, more of originality.

It has been held, and with justice, that in his writing, and hence, by implication, in his thinking, he took too little account of the moral and the spiritual,[2] — that he lacked "ethical insight," what Emerson once charged in effect, but obviously with less of warrant, against Poe's intellectual master, Coleridge;[3] and this defect, it may very well be, limited Poe's influence and his usefulness as a literary critic.

[1] John Macy, *The Spirit of American Literature*, New York, 1913, p. 124. But Mr. Macy overlooks the fact that Poe was personally acquainted with both John Marshall and William Wirt (see *Poe's Works*, VIII, 115; the "Valentine Letters," pp. 125, 131, 133).

[2] Norman Foerster, *American Criticism*, Boston, 1928, p. 14.

[3] *Emerson's Journals*, ed. E. W. Emerson and Waldo Emerson Forbes, Boston, 1910, III, 186.

It has also been said, and again with justice, I think,
that Poe attached too much importance, relatively,
to facts and too little to ideas,[1] — a circumstance ex-
plicable in part, however, by the very nature of the
life he lived, a sort of hand-to-mouth existence affording small opportunity for the more abstract and de-
liberate exercises of the mind in which, under different
conditions, it is at least conceivable that he might
have distinguished himself. It has been held, too,
that his constant repetition of favorite ideas and
situations argues something of intellectual sterility,[2]
and this, likewise, may be conceded; but such a concession should carry with it the further concession
that in his practice of repeating himself he associated
himself with more than one of his most illustrious
compeers in the field of letters.

Question has likewise been raised in some quarters
as to Poe's honesty and his intellectual integrity.
That he was subject to prejudices may at once be
admitted; and it must also be admitted that in his
letters and his reviews he sometimes stooped to inordinate flattery or indulged in a species of literary
log-rolling. In particular, — either by reason of his
chivalry or, it may be, for selfish motives, — he was
given to extravagant praise of certain women who
enjoyed his admiration and whose favor he courted.
But an even more serious indictment has been
brought against him, to the effect that he at times

[1] Paul Elmer More, "A Note on Poe's Method," *Studies in Philology*,
xx, 302 (July, 1923).   [2] Foerster, *American Criticism*, p. 7.

made a display of learning or affected an erudition to which he had no claim. Specifically it is alleged that his erudite lists of out-of-the-way authors and books sometimes involved mere affectation and show, — charlatanry it has been called, — and that his quotations and allusions were often at second hand.[1] And there is no denying that he interlarded his writings too freely with French and Latin quotations, and that he carried too far the use of foot-notes and of learned commentary, — notably in his two longer poems, "Tamerlane" and "Al Aaraaf." But surely too much has been made of his weakness in this direction. Both his citation of out-of-the-way authorities and his use of foreign phrases and quotations he sometimes indulged in deliberately for artistic purposes. The numerous phrases from the French in "Bon-Bon" and "The Duc de L'Omelette," for instance, were introduced for the sake of atmosphere. In "Lionizing" the wealth of learned allusion is a part of Poe's humor. And I cannot feel that the catalogue of strange books in "The Fall of the House of Usher" is out of place. That Poe was not ignorant,

[1] See, for instance, W. C. Brownell, *American Prose Masters*, New York, 1909, p. 249; Joseph W. Krutch, *Edgar Allan Poe*, New York, 1926, pp. 92 f.; Edith Philips, "The French of Edgar Allan Poe," *American Speech*, ii, 270 f. (March, 1927); Carl Schreiber, "Mr. Poe at his Conjurations Again," The *Colophon*, ii, 1 f. (May, 1930); Edwin Greenlaw, "Poe in the Light of Literary History," the *Johns Hopkins Alumni Magazine*, xviii, 276 f. (June, 1930). And see for examples of his borrowing of mottoes and the like from Disraeli, Montgomery, and others, Woodberry, in *Poe's Works*, ed. Stedman and Woodberry, Chicago, 1895, iii, 280 f., and Earl Leslie Griggs, "Five Sources of Edgar Allan Poe's 'Pinakidia,'" *American Literature*, i, 197 f. (May, 1929).

moreover, of the folly of a parade of learning may be inferred from his ridicule of it in "How to Write a Blackwood Article." "To be ignorant of Latin is no crime," he writes in one of his reviews; "to pretend a knowledge is beneath contempt." [1] It may be said, moreover, in partial extenuation of Poe's too prolific use of mottoes and foot-notes, that he was but falling in with a fashion of the day, freely resorted to by Scott and Southey and Byron and Moore among others; and, further, that he made much less of such display in his later years.

IV

I come back, in conclusion, to the query with which I started, the question raised by Lanier's observation: "The trouble with Poe was, he did not *know* enough." The matter is, by its very nature, difficult to settle. The great poet, it goes without saying, will be possessed of wisdom and of insight; but how far learning is necessary to the achievement of greatness with the imaginative writer must, I think, remain a moot point. Poe indeed declares of Coleridge that he went wrong "by reason of his very profundity." [2] And it can at least be said that Lowell's erudition did not invariably stand him in good stead as a poet.

It is perhaps late in the day to be raising any question as to Poe's intellectual powers and attainments. But I have felt that Lanier, writing as he did before

---

[1] *Poe's Works*, XI, 137.   [2] *Ibid.*, VII, xxxix.

any satisfactory edition of Poe's works had been
brought out, was hardly in a position to pass with
full assurance on the poet's intellectual equipment;
and that others have made too much of his occasional
pedantries and affectations; and that quite too much
has been made of his superficialities here and there.
He was not, of course, a scholar, nor professed to be
— nor needed to be. He lacked common sense and
practical wisdom. He was frequently inaccurate, and
he was seldom thorough. His knowledge of some
fields was beyond any question restricted. He had
had, as he would have been ready enough to admit,
little education of a formal sort.[1] But judged by
present-day standards, he possessed an unusually
wide acquaintance with things in general, and in particular with the literature of his own day. He was
not profound; but he did his own thinking, and he
had intellectual courage in plenty. His mind was re-
markably clear; and in powers of analysis I wonder
if he was surpassed by any writer of his day. In
native endowment and in insight he seems to me
to have possessed gifts comparable to those of any
other American writer of his time, save possibly
Emerson. What is much more remarkable than any
intellectual limitations under which he labored is the
fact that, despite these inhibitions and his many
physical handicaps, he managed, by reason of his in-
dustry and his enterprise and his resourcefulness, to
accomplish as much as he did.

[1] See in this connection the "Valentine Letters," p. 253.

CONTEMPORARY OPINION OF POE[1]

I

A DIVERSITY of opinion has been expressed as to Poe's contemporary vogue, but the view has been widely held that he was but little esteemed in his own day. Thus so distinguished a scholar as the late Sir Walter Raleigh, of Oxford, in a letter addressed to the celebrators of the Poe centenary at the University of Virginia (1909), makes the statement that Poe was "barely recognized while he lived." [2] Baudelaire, who did more than any other to light the flame of Poe's reputation abroad, held that Poe had been cruelly neglected by his fellow-countrymen; [3] and a similar view has been held, I believe, by most other Frenchmen. In America, too, there has long existed a tradition that Poe was but little appreciated while he lived, — a tradition that has flourished especially in the South, though it has not been confined to the

---

[1] Reprinted, with revisions and additions, from the *Publications of the Modern Language Association of America*, xxxvi, 142–166 (April, 1921).

[2] *The Book of the Poe Centenary*, ed. Kent and Patton, University of Virginia, 1909, p. 201.

[3] See the essay with which he prefaced his first series of *Histoires Extraordinaires par Edgar Poe*, Paris, 1856.

South.[1] On the other hand, some of the ablest of our students of Poe have held that this tradition is without any substantial basis in fact. The lamented Professor Charles F. Richardson, for instance, in one of the most sympathetic and discriminating essays that we have on the Southern poet, asserts that it is "a serious mistake" to assume that Poe was unpopular in his own day.[2] And Professor W. P. Trent, a no less eminent authority on our literary history, has recorded the belief that "Poe is no exception to the rule that the writers who really count began by counting with their contemporaries."[3]

With a view to ascertaining the facts in the case — of discovering, if possible, just what the attitude of Poe's contemporaries toward him was — I have entertained myself at off hours by collecting from the periodicals of Poe's time the principal comments on his work that I have come across in the course of my browsings. I have also taken account of such contemporary evidence as I chanced to find in letters and other manuscripts belonging to this period, and likewise of the chief critical judgments called out by

[1] For echoes of this tradition see John R. Thompson in the *Southern Literary Messenger*, xv, 694 (November, 1849); J. M. Daniel, *ibid.*, xvi, 184 (March, 1850); J. H. Hewitt, *Shadows on the Wall*, Baltimore, 1877, p. 41; C. L. Moore, in the *Dial*, xxvi, 40 (January 16, 1899); and the New York *Times*, August 11, 1918, p. 348 (an editorial in which the statement is made that Poe "fought a hopeless struggle against contemporary coldness and inappreciation").

[2] *Poe's Works*, ed. Richardson, i, xviii.

[3] *Longfellow and Other Essays*, New York [1910], p. 218. See also Macy, *The Spirit of American Literature*, New York, 1913, p. 127, and Woodberry in the *Century Magazine*, xlviii, 866 (October, 1894).

Poe's death and by the publication of his collected works.[1] Naturally I have confined myself mainly to American periodicals,[2] but I have also taken account of the more significant among the contemporary foreign criticisms that have come under my notice.[3]

The conclusions which these contemporary judg-

[1] *The Works of the Late Edgar Allan Poe*, ed. R. W. Griswold, New York, 1850, 1856.

[2] Among the American periodicals that I have examined are the *Southern Literary Messenger*, the Richmond *Enquirer* (1826–1828, 1835–1837), the Richmond *Whig* (1835–1837, 1848–1849), the Richmond *Examiner* (1849), the Baltimore *Minerva and Emerald* (1829–1830), the Baltimore *Republican* (1831–1835), the Baltimore *American* (1832–1837), the Baltimore *Patriot* (1832–1837), the Baltimore *Weekly Gazette* (1832–1834), the Baltimore *Young Men's Paper* (1835), the Baltimore *American Museum*, the Baltimore *Saturday Visiter* (1832–1834, 1841–1846), Atkinson's Philadelphia *Casket* (1827–1840), the *Saturday Evening Post* (1829–1833, 1839–1840, 1850), the Philadelphia *Saturday Courier* (1831–1852), *Godey's Lady's Book*, the *American Monthly Review*, the *North American Magazine*, *Burton's Gentleman's Magazine*, *Graham's Magazine*, *Alexander's Weekly Messenger* (1837–1838), the Philadelphia *United States Gazette* (1839–1844), the *Dollar Newspaper*, the *Dollar Magazine* (1840–1841), the Philadelphia *Spirit of the Times* (1845–1847), Peterson's *National Magazine* (1845–1847, 1853), the New York *Mirror*, the New York *Review*, the *American Whig Review*, the *Democratic Review*, the *Columbian Magazine*, the *New World*, Post's *Union Magazine*, Sartain's *Union Magazine*, the *Home Journal* (1846–1860), the *Literary World* (1847–1853), the *Nineteenth Century* (1848–1849), Snowden's *Ladies' Companion*, the *Broadway Journal*, *Holden's Dollar Magazine* (1849), the New York *Tribune* (1845–1846, 1849–1850), the *Knickerbocker* (1827–1855), the *Brother Jonathan* (1842–1843), the *North American Review* (1827–1860), the *Dial*, the *Pioneer*, the *New England Magazine*, the *New Englander*, the *Waverley Magazine* (1853), the Boston *Notion* (1843), the *Yankee and Boston Literary Gazette* (1827–1829), the Pittsburgh *Literary Examiner* (1839), the *Western Quarterly Review* (1849), and the Washington *National Intelligencer* (1845–1847).

[3] Studies of Poe's vogue and influence in France have been made by Professor G. D. Morris in his *Fenimore Cooper et Edgar Poe*, Paris, 1912, pp. 67–208, and by Professor C. P. Cambiaire in his *The Influence of Edgar Allan Poe in France*, New York, 1927.

ments seem to warrant may be summarized as follows:

1. That as poet Poe was not held in very high esteem by his contemporaries, and that he was all but ignored until after the publication of "The Raven" in 1845.

2. That as a writer of gruesome and fantastical tales he early achieved considerable local fame, and that before his death he had come to be generally recognized as one of the leading writers of short stories in America.

3. That it was as a critic that he was chiefly known in his day in America, though as a fearless and caustic and not always impartial critic rather than as a just and discriminating critic.

4. That his early reputation abroad, however, rested almost solely on his work as poet and romancer.

II

Poe's first two volumes of poetry, the editions of 1827 and 1829,[1] — his first publications of any sort, so far as is now known, — appear to have fallen still-born from the press. There were, it seems, no reviews of the volume of 1827, the only public notice that appeared at the time being, apparently, the bare mention of the title in the monthly book-lists of two New

---

[1] *Tamerlane and Other Poems*, Boston, 1827; *Al Aaraaf, Tamerlane, and Minor Poems*, Baltimore, 1829.

England magazines [1] and in the "Catalogue of American Poetry" compiled by Kettell in his *Specimens of American Literature*.[2] And the only reviews of the second of these volumes that have come to my attention are the well-known advance notice published by John Neal in the *Yankee and Boston Literary Gazette* for December, 1829, a perfunctory judgment based mainly on excerpts from "Al Aaraaf" and "Tamerlane," [3] and a more discriminating notice, attributed to Mrs. Sarah Josepha Hale, published in the Boston *Ladies' Magazine* for January, 1830 (see J. H. Whitty in the New York *Evening Post*, August 13, 1921). There were, however, two contemporary notices of "Fairy-Land," which appeared in the volume of 1829, that will serve to indicate the attitude of the press toward Poe. John Neal, in printing the poem in the *Yankee*, observes that, "though nonsense," it is at least "exquisite nonsense"; [4] while N. P. Willis in the *American Monthly Magazine* for November, 1829,[5] in editorially rejecting the poem for publication, describes it as "some sickly rhymes."

Of Poe's third volume of verses, published in 1831 and containing among other things "Israfel," "The

---

[1] The *United States Review and Literary Gazette*, ii, 379 (August, 1927); the *North American Review*, xxv, 471 (October, 1927).

[2] iii, 405. Published at Boston in 1829.

[3] The *Yankee and Boston Literary Gazette*, iii, 295–298.

[4] *Ibid.*, p. 168.

[5] i, 586–587. The volume of 1829 is said to have been reviewed by J. H. Hewitt in the Baltimore *Minerva and Emerald* (see Hewitt's *Shadows on the Wall*, p. 41), but I have been unable to find this notice in any issue of the *Emerald* for 1830.

City in the Sea," and the early lyric "To Helen," there was a brief notice in the Philadelphia *Casket* for May, 1831,[1] and a longer and more sympathetic notice, apparently by George P. Morris, in the New York *Mirror* of May 7, 1831, the reviewer observing that the language employed revealed "poetic inspiration" and that some of the lyrics possessed "a plausible air of imagination," but that the volume exhibited a "general indefiniteness of the ideas," "numerous obscurities," and an occasional "conflict of beauty and nonsense." [2]

In Cheever's *American Commonplace Book of Poetry* (1831) Poe's name did not appear among the three score poets there represented, and he was similarly ignored in several magazine articles on American poetry published in the thirties.[3] Here and there in the *Southern Literary Messenger* during the period of Poe's connection with it (1835–1837), one stumbles upon some word of comment on stray poems of his published there; but these notices are invariably lacking in warmth; and it is plain that neither Thomas W. White [4] (the proprietor of the *Messenger*) nor any of his literary advisers, among whom he counted

[1] v, 289–290.

[2] The New York *Mirror*, VIII, 349–350.

[3] See the *Edinburgh Review*, LXI, 12–21 (April, 1835); the *Southern Literary Messenger*, IV, 85 (February, 1838); and the review of Cheever's book in the *North American Review*, XXXIII, 297–324 (October, 1831).

[4] See the *Messenger* for April, 1835 (I, 460), December, 1835 (II, 1), September, 1839 (V, 708), January, 1840 (VI, 126), September, 1840 (VI, 707–710), April, 1841 (VII, 310–313), July, 1841 (VII, 592).

Beverly Tucker and John Pendleton Kennedy,[1] had any just conception of Poe's capabilities as a poet.

A similar neglect attended the poet through his first New York period (1837–1838) and his Philadelphia period (1838–1844). He was not mentioned by Keese in his *Poets of America* (1838), nor by Bryant in his *Selections from the American Poets* (1840); and Griswold in his voluminous anthology, *The Poets and Poetry of America* (1842), included only three of his poems, although he made room for upwards of a dozen from Pierpont and more than a score from Percival. In a review of Griswold's anthology by John Forster (biographer of Dickens) in 1844, Poe is held to possess genuine gifts as artist and something of spirituality, but to be too obviously imitative.[2] Henry B. Hirst, to be sure, in his sketch of Poe in the *Saturday Museum* of February 25, 1843, praises him at some length, declaring his poems to be "remarkable for vigor, terseness, brilliancy, and for their chaste and finished style"; but little importance attaches to a judgment proceeding from so undisguised a tool as Hirst was at that time.

The first contemporary notice of any importance in which Poe is conceded to possess more than ordinary merit as poet is that of James Russell Lowell in *Graham's Magazine* for February, 1845 [3] (published

[1] For Kennedy's references to Poe, see Woodberry, *Life of Poe*, I, 109–110, 141–142, 148–149.

[2] The *Foreign Quarterly Review*, XXXII, 321–322 (January, 1844).

[3] XXVII, 49–53.

before January 29).[1] In a letter to Poe of May 8, 1843, Lowell had written: "Your early poems display a maturity which astonished me & I recollect no individual . . . whose early poems were anything like as good."[2] In his notice in *Graham's*[3] he reiterates this judgment, and then goes on to praise Poe's lyrics for their melody, for their felicity of diction, and for the "fecundity of imagination" displayed by them, remarking of "The Haunted Palace" that he knew "no modern poet who might not have been justly proud of it."

With the publication of "The Raven," some ten days after the first publication of Lowell's article, Poe came to enjoy for the time being a country-wide notoriety. The poem was copied far and wide in the press of America, and was generously received in England. Mrs. Browning wrote from London in 1846 that it had "produced a sensation" in England.[4] Willis pronounced it, on its first publication, "the most effective single example of 'fugitive poetry' ever published" in America. Briggs, who was presently to turn against Poe, described it in the *Broadway Journal* of February 8, 1845, as "a piece of verse which the best of our poets would hardly wish to disown." A contributor to the New York *Tribune* of February 3, 1845, — possibly Horace Greeley, — declared that it would have "enriched *Blackwood*."

---

[1] On which date it was reprinted in the *Evening Mirror*.
[2] Woodberry, *Life of Poe*, II, 27.
[3] XXVII, 51, 52.
[4] *Poe's Works*, XVII, 229.

And the writer of a brief sketch of Poe in the Philadelphia *Saturday Courier* of July 25, 1846, remarked that "no American poem, for many years, has attracted, on both sides of the water, so much attention from the literary, critical, and general reader."

But "The Raven," despite its extraordinary reception, was powerless to establish for Poe an enduring hold on the poetry-reading public of his time; for when it reappeared in the fall of 1845 as the title-piece in a collective edition of Poe's poetical works, the reviews were prevailingly unsympathetic. There was no notice of the volume in *Graham's*, or in the *Whig Review*, or in the *North American Review*, and the notices in the *Mirror* (November 29, 1845) and the *Democratic Review* (December, 1845, and March, 1847) were brief. Margaret Fuller wrote in the New York *Tribune* (November 26, 1845) that "The Raven" was a "rare and finished specimen," but was apparently intended "chiefly to show the writer's artistic skill." Reviews in the *Knickerbocker* (January, 1846)[1] and the London *Literary Gazette* (March 14, 1846) were wholly adverse, Lewis Gaylord Clark in the *Knickerbocker* savagely remarking of the poems in their entirety that he saw "no reason why they might not have been written at the age of ten."

During the remaining years of his life — 1846 to 1849 — Poe's reputation as poet underwent little change. "Ulalume," like "The Raven," went begging at first for a publisher;[2] an improved draft of

---

[1] xxvii, 69. [2] See Stoddard, *Poe's Works*, New York [1884], i, 150.

"The Bells" was held in the editorial drawers of *Sartain's* for nine months before publication; and most of Poe's other poems belonging to this period were sold to an obscure Boston weekly, the *Flag of Our Union*, with which the poet confessed to Willis he was ashamed to have any connection.[1] There was favorable mention of the poems in P. P. Cooke's continuation of Lowell's sketch in 1848;[2] Lowell himself, in the same year, though he had lost faith in Poe as a man, generously pronounced him, in that most famous of all contemporary judgments, to be "three fifths . . . genius"; Willis stood ready to puff any new poem as it appeared; and Griswold on publishing revised editions of his *Poets and Poetry of America* admitted a larger and larger number of his poems, until a total of fourteen was reached in the year of Poe's death. But the public, in so far as it was interested in Poe at this time, was mainly concerned with his prose writings and with certain regrettable lapses in his personal conduct that marked this period of his career.

During the decade immediately following the poet's death there were numberless articles in the American press dealing with his life and work, and there were articles also in a dozen of the English magazines. These differed widely in their appraisal of his work as poet, but they contained little wholehearted commendation. "All his poetry . . . was mere

[1] *Poe's Works*, XVII, 351.
[2] The *Southern Literary Messenger*, XIV, 34–38 (January, 1848).

machine work," wrote Briggs in *Holden's Dollar Magazine*.[1] Ripley, in the New York *Tribune*,[2] declared that the "prevailing characteristic" of his poems "was an extreme artificiality." Griswold, while praising the construction of his poems, objected that they evinced "little genuine feeling" and displayed "an absence of all impulse."[3] "He perpetually reminds us of something we have read before," observed the writer of an extended notice in the *Edinburgh Review*[4] in discussing his poems. And Chivers, in 1853, ruthlessly charged Poe with having pilfered from his strangely unequal jingles materials used in "The Raven" and other lyrics.[5] Daniel, the Richmond editor and diplomat, wrote in the *Southern Literary Messenger* of March, 1850:[6] "Among all his poems, there are only two or three which are not execrably bad." "Few of his poems . . . will live with his land and language," declared Savage in the *Democratic Review* for February, 1851.[7] Stoddard wrote, in the *National Magazine* of April, 1853:[8] "Save the 'Raven,' and one or two similar poems, the sooner the mass of [his poetry] dies the better for his reputation."

Among the scattering notices commendatory of Poe as poet may be mentioned an article in *Chambers's*

[1] iv, 765 (December, 1849).

[2] January 17, 1850.

[3] See his edition of *Poe's Works*, iii, xlviii.

[4] cvii, 426 (April, 1858).

[5] The *Waverley Magazine*, July 30, September 10, and October 1, 1853.

[6] xiv, 172.   [7] xxviii, 171.   [8] ii, 199.

Edinburgh Journal (February 26, 1853), in which it is
asserted that Poe was "unquestionably the most original imaginative writer America has yet produced,"
and that "there is not a line in all his poetry which
suggests the idea of imitation"; a notice by Willis in
the *Home Journal* (October 27, 1849), in which he
declared that "The Bells," together with "The
Raven," "Ulalume," and "The Haunted Palace,"
afforded "unquestionably titles to an enduring reputation"; [1] a chapter by Powell in his *Living Authors
of America* (p. 121), in which the opinion was expressed that "in a few years" Poe would be "considered one of America's best poets"; and an essay
by Leigh Hunt in the *North British Review* (August,
1852),[2] in which he gave it as his opinion that Poe was
one of the four "most notable [poets] as yet produced by America."

But no one can read the contemporary judgments
on Poe without being convinced that he had not, at
the time of his death, established himself in the minds
of his countrymen as a poet of extraordinary worth; [3]

[1] See the article of T. O. Mabbott in *Modern Language Notes*, xxxv,
373 (June, 1920).

[2] xviii, 395.

[3] The attitude of Poe's fellow-craftsmen in America appears to have
been much the same as that of the reading public at large. Both Lowell
and Willis, as we have seen, early accepted Poe as a poet of exceptional
ability. Whittier, in later years, ungrudgingly conceded to him the gift
of genius (see a letter of September 21, 1875, published in Gill's *Life of
Poe*, p. 284). But Emerson was unable to see in Poe anything more than
a facile rhymester, a "jingle man," and was careful to omit him from his
American *Parnassus* (1874). Bryant excluded him, as we have seen,
from his *Selections from the American Poets* (1840), and in his *Library of
Poetry and Song* (1871) admitted only four of his poems ("The Raven,"

and it is equally plain that he had not attained any
considerable vogue in foreign lands.[1]

"Annabel Lee," "The Bells," and "For Annie"). Longfellow, while
recognizing in him a man richly endowed both as poet and as prose
writer (see the *Southern Literary Messenger*, xv, 696), thought of him,
apparently, as a romancer first of all rather than as a poet (see a letter of
his believed to have been addressed to Poe, quoted in part in Catalogue
No. 27 of Robert H. Dodd, March, 1918, p. 8). Whitman, like Emerson,
was disposed to think of Poe as a juggler of words and as overfond of the
spectacular and the gruesome, — though he came to think better of him
in later years. See a statement made to Traubel (*With Walt Whitman in
Camden*, III, 138–139) in 1888: "Do I like Poe? At the start for many
years, not: but three or four years ago I got to reading him again, reading
and liking, until at last — yes, now — I feel almost convinced that he is
a star of considerable magnitude, if not a sun, in the literary firmament."
Simms wrote to Chivers in 1852: "He was a man of curious genius, wild
and erratic, but his genius was rather curious than valuable — bizarre,
rather than great or healthful" (the *Century Magazine*, LXV, 552); and
George William Curtis wrote Mrs. Whitman in 1846: "I should much
like to see anything really good of [Poe's]" (the *Atlantic Monthly*, CXIV,
372).

Bryant, after Emerson, among all the American poets, appears to
have had least admiration for Poe, being blinded, I suspect, by his belief
that Poe was a bad man. To Miss S. S. Rice, of Baltimore, then engaged
in an effort to raise funds for a memorial to Poe in that city, he wrote on
November 6, 1865: "I am very unwilling to do anything which may seem
disobliging, yet I cannot comply with the request in your note. . . . My
difficulty arises from the personal character of Edgar A. Poe, of which I
have in my time heard too much to be able to join in paying especial
honor to his memory. Persons younger than myself who have heard less
of the conduct to which I refer may take a different view of the matter,
and, certainly, I do not intend to censure them for doing so. I think,
however, that there should be some decided element of goodness in the
character of those to whom a public monument directs the attention of
the world" (the Baltimore *Sun*, January 17, 1909).

[1] But see the article of A. Yarmolinsky in the New York *Bookman*,
September, 1916 (XLIV, 44 f.), in which we learn that translations of
certain of Poe's writings appeared in Russian periodicals "as early as
the late thirties." For Poe's contemporary reputation in France, see
G. D. Morris, *Fenimore Cooper et Edgar Poe*, pp. 80 ff., and C. P. Cambiaire, *The Influence of Edgar Allan Poe in France*, pp. 13 ff.; and for his
vogue in Germany, F. Hippe, *Edgar Allan Poes Lyrik in Deutschland*,
Münster, 1913, pp. 13 ff.

III

As a writer of tales Poe fared a good deal better with his contemporaries than he did as a poet. The first of his tales to be published, so far as we know, were five stories submitted in competition for a prize offered by the Philadelphia *Saturday Courier* in 1831.[1] These were published anonymously, in the *Courier* for 1832, and apparently attracted little if any attention, the prize being awarded (as an ironical fate would have it) to Delia Bacon. He was more successful, however, in his competition for a prize offered in 1833 by the Baltimore *Saturday Visiter*, winning this prize and receiving at the same time the public commendation of the judges, — John Pendleton Kennedy being one of their number, — who in making their official report [2] pronounced his tales to be "eminently distinguished by a wild, vigorous, and poetical imagination, a rich style, a fertile invention, and varied and curious learning," and to be "very creditable to the rising literature of our country." A year before this the editor of the *Visiter* (in its issue of August 4, 1832) had remarked of a manuscript volume of his tales submitted to him by Poe that "for originality, richness of imagery and purity of the style, few American authors in our opinion have produced any-

---

[1] See my article in the *Dial* for February 17, 1916.

[2] Duly published in the *Visiter* of October 12, 1833 (see the article of Professor J. C. French, in *Modern Language Notes*, XXXIII, 260 f. [May, 1918]). See, also, the slightly garbled version of this in the *Southern Literary Messenger*, I, 716 (August, 1835).

thing superior." And after his assumption of an editorial position with the *Southern Literary Messenger* in 1835, notices of his stories came thick and fast. In these notices — which were industriously collected by the proprietor of the *Messenger*, and published in appendixes to certain issues of the magazine[1] — there was liberal praise of his early work as a writer of stories. Praise was also forthcoming through the medium of personal letters. Kennedy wrote, in introducing Poe to White, that the "young fellow" was "highly imaginative" (though "a little given to the terrific").[2] Paulding wrote in 1836: "Mr. Poe [is] decidedly the best of all our young writers; I don't know but I might add all our old ones, with one or two exceptions."[3] And Beverly Tucker expressed the opinion as early as November, 1835, that Poe had "been already praised as much as was good for him."[4] Dispraise, such as there was, rested on the ground of his extravagance, the excess of the "unnatural and the horrible," of "German enchantment and supernatural imagery."

On the other hand, American publishers, both at this time and later, were chary of bringing out any collection of Poe's tales, H. C. Carey (on behalf of Carey and Lea) explaining in a letter to Kennedy of November 26, 1834, that the demand for such "little things" was slight and the "produce" from them

[1] II, 133 ff., 341 ff., 517 ff. (January, April, July, 1836).
[2] Woodberry, *Life of Poe*, I, 110.
[3] The *Southern Literary Messenger*, II, 138 (January, 1836).
[4] Woodberry, I, 152.

"small." [1] Nevertheless, the Harpers were prevailed upon in 1838 to publish his longer story, *The Narrative of Arthur Gordon Pym*, and the next year Carey and Lea brought out a two-volume collection of his stories, *Tales of the Grotesque and Arabesque*.

Pym was but indifferently received, L. G. Clark, in the *Knickerbocker* for August, 1838,[2] complaining that the style was "loose and slip-shod" and that the plot was "too liberally stuffed with 'horrid circumstance of blood and battle'"; while Burton, in his *Gentleman's Magazine* for September, 1838,[3] expressed regret at finding Poe's name "in connection with such a mass of ignorance and effrontery," and declared contemptuously that "a more impudent attempt at humbugging the public [had] never been exercised."

But the *Tales of the Grotesque and Arabesque*, although the volumes had at first very small sale (less than 750 copies being disposed of during the first three years after publication),[4] appears to have been warmly received by the New York and Philadelphia papers.[5] Among the notices that appeared at this

---

[1] The *Sewanee Review*, xxv, 197 (April, 1917).   [2] xii, 167.

[3] iii, 211. A notice in like vein also appeared in the New York *Mirror*, August 11, 1838. From a letter from Harper and Brothers of February 20, 1839 (preserved among the Griswold Papers), it appears that less than a hundred copies of it were sold in America during the first year after publication, though it seems to have fared somewhat better in England.

[4] See the communication of Henry C. Lea to the New York *Nation*, xxxi, 408 (December 9, 1880).

[5] See the sheaf of complimentary notices collected at the back of the second volume of certain copies of the *Tales of the Grotesque and Arabesque*; and see also a letter of Poe's of December 19, 1839 (Woodberry, i, 238).

time was a highly complimentary review, by L. F. Tasistro, in the New York *Mirror*, which, inasmuch as it is one of the soundest contemporary judgments on Poe, may be quoted at some length.

Had Mr. Poe written nothing else but "Morella," "William Wilson," "The House of Usher," and the "MS. Found in a Bottle," he would deserve a high place among imaginative writers, for there is fine poetic feeling, much brightness of fancy, an excellent taste, a ready eye for the picturesque, much quickness of observation, and great truth of sentiment and character in all of these works. But there is scarcely one of the tales published in the two volumes before us, in which we do not find the development of great intellectual capacity, with a power for vivid description, an opulence of imagination, a fecundity of invention, and a command over the elegances of diction which have seldom been displayed, even by writers who have acquired the greatest distinction in the republic of letters.[1]

The poet's heart was made glad, also, about this time by two complimentary letters from Washington Irving, to whom he had sent copies of some of his stories, Irving assuring him that the "graphic effect" of "The Fall of the House of Usher" was "powerful," and that "William Wilson" possessed a "singular and mysterious interest" that was "well sustained throughout." [2]

[1] New York *Mirror*, XVII, 215 (December 28, 1839).
[2] See Woodberry, I, 216 f., and the notices appended to the second volume of the *Tales of the Grotesque and Arabesque*. Cf. also a complimentary reference by Willis in his *Letters from Under a Bridge*, London, 1840, p. 121.

Further impetus was given to the growth of Poe's fame as a romancer by his success in 1843 in winning, with his extraordinarily fine tale, "The Gold-Bug," a prize of a hundred dollars offered by the Philadelphia *Dollar Newspaper*. Of this tale Poe made the claim a year later that over 300,000 copies had been put in circulation.[1]

His reputation as a writer of stories was doubtless overshadowed, in a measure, in 1845 by the sensation caused by the publication of "The Raven." To his friend F. W. Thomas he wrote in May, 1845, with reference to the comparative popularity of "The Raven" and "The Gold-Bug," that "the bird beat the bug . . . all hollow." [2] He succeeded, nevertheless, in finding a publisher, in the summer of 1845, for a new edition of his tales. And this, too, was well received. The volume was reviewed at length in the *American Whig Review* of September, 1845,[3] being there pronounced "one of the most original and peculiar ever published in the United States," and was warmly praised also in *Graham's Magazine* (September, 1845) [4] and by Thomas Dunn English in the *Aristidean*.[5] There were notices, also, in the foreign press — by Martin Farquhar Tupper in the London *Literary Gazette* of January 31, 1846; by E. D. Forgues in the *Revue des deux Mondes* of October 15, 1846; [6] and by an anonymous reviewer (hardly Christopher

---

[1] Woodberry, II, 70. Whether Poe's statement is to be accepted at face value is questionable.

[2] *Ibid.*, p. 135. [3] II, 306–309. [4] XXVIII, 143.

[5] I, 316 ff. (October, 1845). [6] XVI, 341–366.

North) in *Blackwood's* for November, 1847 [1] — each of which, though guarded in its praise of the volume as a whole, freely commended Poe's power of analysis.

Among other contemporary judgments the most important is that of Lowell, who in his article in *Graham's* [2] declared, with obvious reference to the tales, that Poe possessed "a faculty of vigorous yet minute analysis and a wonderful fecundity of imagination," together with a "highly finished, graceful and truly classical" style. Important also is an article on the tale-writers of America by Rufus W. Griswold, in the Washington *National Intelligencer* of August 30, 1845, in which Poe was given a place in the forefront of American tale-writers, and was held to possess "a great deal of imagination and fancy" and to be a "consummate artist." Griswold also wrote in praise of Poe in his *Prose Writers of America* (1847), declaring there his belief that it was as a writer of tales that Poe had "most reputation." Hawthorne, also, testified at this time to his belief in Poe's genius as a tale-writer, assuring him in a letter written in 1846 that he "could never fail to recognize [the] force and originality" of his stories.[3] On the other hand, the *North American Review*, in noticing Simms's novels in 1846, incidentally refers to the 1845 volume of Poe's tales as "belonging to the forcible-feeble and the shallow-profound school," a judgment that was copied into the *Knickerbocker* with

[1] LXII, 582–587.   [2] XXVII, 51, 52 (February, 1845).
[3] *Poe's Works*, XVII, 233.

evident relish on the part of its editor.[1] And in a notice of the *Tales* copied in *Littell's Living Age* for November 15, 1845 (No. 79, p. 343), an anonymous English writer, while admitting that Poe "could not possibly send forth a book without some marks of his genius," complains that "Mr. Poe's *Tales* are out of place," and queries, "Why has Mr. Poe given us so much of the scraps and the worn-out thoughts of yesterday?"

Most of the notices published after Poe's death spoke in praise of the tales. Henry B. Hirst in the *Saturday Courier* of October 20, 1849, declared that Poe was "unrivalled as a tale-writer." Savage in the *Democratic Review*[2] ventured the prophecy that "as a prose writer he [would] go down to posterity with the full tide of reputation." Lewis Gaylord Clark, in spite of his inveterate enmity to Poe, admitted that he possessed exceptional "constructive faculty," "remarkable ingenuity," and "vivid imagination."[3] Others emphasized his originality.[4] Baudelaire in his famous sketch of 1856 dwelt on his gifts as artist, and in common with French critics of a later period made much of his powers of analysis.[5] Stoddard in the *National Magazine* (March, 1853)[6] spoke of him as a

[1] The *North American Review*, LXIII, 359 (October, 1846); the *Knicker-bocker*, XXVIII, 452 (November, 1846).

[2] XXVIII, 171 (February, 1851).

[3] The *Knickerbocker*, XXXV, 163 (February, 1850).

[4] See Powell, *Living Authors of America*, New York, 1850, p. 132; G. W. Peck in the *American Whig Review*, XI, 307 (March, 1850); Gil-fillan, *A Third Gallery of Portraits*, Edinburgh, 1854, pp. 380 ff.

[5] *Histoires Extraordinaires par Edgar Poe*, pp. 28 ff.

[6] II, 198.

"profound artist," and expressed the opinion that "The Fall of the House of Usher" was "the most admirable thing of the kind in the whole range of English literature." Powell,[1] who conceded to Poe the gift of genius,[2] expressed the belief that he would after a few years "chiefly be remembered for his tales." [3]

IV

But it was as critic, as I have said, that Poe was best known to his contemporaries in America. By this I do not mean that his book-reviews and other critical papers were felt to exceed in importance his poems or his tales: the consensus of intelligent opinion would have given first place in the matter of actual worth

[1] *Living Authors of America*, p. 134.

[2] Lowell also had pronounced Poe a genius in his article in *Graham's* in 1845 (xxvii, 52), and this judgment remained unaltered in the revised form of his essay published in the Griswold edition of Poe's works (iii, xii). Others who spoke of him in similar terms were Ripley (the New York *Tribune* for January 17, 1850), Gilfillan (*A Third Gallery of Portraits*, p. 380), and John M. Daniel (the *Southern Literary Messenger*, xvi, 172). But it is fairly plain that no one of these, except possibly Lowell, employed the word "genius" with the meaning that we commonly attach to it at the present time. Daniel, in his slashing way, while condemning Poe as a poet, assigns him the foremost place among American writers (*ibid.*, p. 178), — though he does not make it clear whether he bases this judgment on his tales or on his critical and philosophical writings: at one point (*ibid.*, p. 181) he asserts that *Eureka* was his "greatest work."

[3] Of adverse criticisms that were made at the time, Duyckinck and Daniel complained of the lack of reality in the tales and of Poe's "want of sympathy with the human kind"; Peck admitted that some of the tales were "too horrible"; Stoddard maintained that his tales were "by no means healthy." Others complained of Poe's lack of humor. And from Clark and Griswold there went up the old cry of plagiarism, notably in the case of "The Pit and the Pendulum."

to his tales. Nevertheless, it is clear from the contemporary references to Poe that it was as critic and book-reviewer that he was most widely known to his generation in America: the mention of his name brought to the minds of his fellow-Americans of the thirties and forties of last century the idea, first of all, of book-reviewer and editor, rather than of tale-writer or of poet.

It does not affect the validity of this assertion to add that Poe was chiefly known as a fearless and caustic critic, rather than as a just and discriminating critic. Indeed, we shall find, I think, in the boldness and the occasional severity of his critical notices the secret of much of his contemporary vogue; for then, as now, it was the controversial and the spectacular that most readily caught the public fancy. And Poe's criticisms, though far more just than his contemporaries could have brought themselves to admit, were in no small degree controversial in nature, — or, at best, calculated to arouse controversy, — and were from the beginning more caustic, I imagine, than anything that had preceded them in American letters.

As in the case of his tales, it was during his connection with the *Southern Literary Messenger* (1835–1837) that he first came into prominence as a critic. Where or when he had served his apprenticeship as a book-reviewer, we shall probably never know. There is no tangible evidence that he had published anything in the way of criticism before 1835, save the "Letter to B——" in the *Poems* of 1831. But by the end of his first year with the *Messenger* he had won for that magazine a place among the leading American critical journals and had brought about an increase in its list of subscribers but little short of miraculous.[1] His tales contributed in good part, no doubt, to this result, but it was his book-reviews and his scorching editorials that were mainly responsible; and it was these, even more than the tales, that attracted the newspaper critics of the time.[2]

His reputation as critic seems to have undergone some arrest in its development during his connection with *Burton's Gentleman's Magazine* in 1839–1840, owing, as he would have had us believe, to the "milk-and-water" policy of its proprietor. But he won fresh laurels for himself while editor of *Graham's Magazine* (1841–1842), writing now some of the ablest of his critiques and earning for himself the almost uniform commendation of the Philadelphia press. Graham, in announcing his accession to his editorial staff, spoke of him as "a stern, just, and impartial critic" who held "a pen second to none in the country";[3] Lowell wrote in praise of his critical work as early as 1842;[4] and Dr. J. Evans Snodgrass, a Balti-

---

[1] The *Broadway Journal*, I, 183 (March 22, 1845); *Poe's Works*, XII, 85.

[2] See the lists of newspaper notices printed in the *Messenger* in 1836 (II, 133 ff., 341 ff., 517 ff.), and see also the opening of his article on the poems of Drake and Halleck in the *Messenger* for April, 1836 (*Poe's Works*, VIII, 275 ff.), and his reply to his critics in the *Messenger* of July, 1836 (*ibid.*, pp. 333 ff.).

[3] The *Saturday Evening Post*, February 20, 1841.

[4] Woodberry, I, 345.

more editor of ability, declared in 1843 that his book-reviews were "unequalled in this country."[1]

As critic Poe also came prominently before the public in 1845 and 1846. During most of 1845 he was either assistant editor or editor of the *Broadway Journal*, and in that capacity wrote, each week, critiques of the more important books appearing at that time. In the spring and summer of 1846 he published in *Godey's Lady's Book* his *Literati*. Of his reviews in the *Broadway Journal* some were very able; but in a number of his papers published there, notably the articles attacking Longfellow, and likewise in the *Literati*, he stooped to personalities of various sorts and displayed a spitefulness that cost him the esteem of some of his staunchest admirers and earned for him the disapproval of most of the influential men of the time. Indeed, the unhappy reputation that he made by these papers he found it impossible to live down during the few remaining years allotted to him.

After 1846 he wrote nothing of importance as critic save "The Poetic Principle," itself a revision in part of work earlier done.

In the notices of Poe published during his lifetime the trait in his criticisms that was most dwelt on was his severity. Before the end of the first year on the *Messenger* he had been taken to task by one of the Richmond newspapers for his "regular cutting and slashing";[2] and he had been attacked earlier in the

[1] The Baltimore *Saturday Visiter*, July 29, 1843.
[2] See Poe's letter to the Richmond *Compiler* of September 2, 1836; reprinted in *Poe's Works*, viii, xii–xv.

year by the New York *Mirror*,[1] in a satirical squib in which he figured as "Bulldog, the critick." Burton reproached him in 1839 for the sharpness of his critical notices in the *Gentleman's Magazine*.[2] Dr. Snodgrass described him in 1842 as "provokingly hypercritical at times";[3] and in a notice of the *Broadway Journal* in April, 1845, he remarked that it "would be more significant to call this the Broad-axe Journal."[4] George D. Prentice violently attacked the poet in 1843 in consequence of his contemptuous references to Carlyle.[5] And Clark, who had been "used up" in the *Literati*, kept up a continual fire at him for a year or more after these papers began to appear. In the *Knickerbocker* of May, 1846, he speaks of Poe as "'*The Literary Snob*' continually obtruding himself upon public notice; to-day, in the gutter, to-morrow in some milliner's magazine; but in all places, and at all times magnificently snobbish and dirty."[6]

Lowell suggested in his sketch in *Graham's*[7] that Poe sometimes mistook "his phial of prussic acid for his ink-stand"; and he rebuked him in his *Fable for Critics* for throwing mudballs at Longfellow. The *Brook Farm Harbinger* in 1845[8] lamented the fact that Poe had taken to a sort of "blackguard warfare."

---

[1] XIII, 324–325 (April 9, 1836).   [2] Woodberry, I, 241.
[3] The Baltimore *Saturday Visiter*, April 2, 1842.
[4] *Ibid.*, April 26, 1845.
[5] See the *Knickerbocker*, XXII, 392 (October, 1843).
[6] *Ibid.*, XXVII, 461.
[7] XXVII, 49–50.   [8] December 6, 1845, p. 410

A contributor to the *Talisman and Odd Fellow's Magazine* in September, 1846,[1] dubbed him "the tomahawk man" and "the Comanche of literature"; and the Philadelphia editor, Du Solle, remarked in 1847, "If Mr. P. had not been gifted with considerable gall, he would have been devoured long ago by the host of enemies his genius has created." [2] In *Holden's Dollar Magazine* for January, 1849 (then edited by C. F. Briggs), Poe is ridiculed in the following doggerel lines: [3]

> With tomahawk upraised for deadly blow,
> Behold our literary Mohawk, Poe!
> Sworn tyrant he o'er all who sin in verse —
> His own the standard, damns he all that's worse;
> And surely not for this shall he be blamed —
> For worse than his deserves that it be damned!

> Who can so well detect the plagiary's flaw?
> "Set thief to catch thief" is an ancient saw:
> Who can so scourge a fool to shreds and slivers?
> Promoted slaves oft make the best slave drivers!
> Iambic Poe! of tyro bards the terror —
> *Ego* is he — the world his pocket-mirror!

[1] I, 105.

[2] The Philadelphia *Spirit of the Times*, January 8, 1847.

[3] III, 22; from a poem entitled "A Mirror for Authors" and dealing, somewhat in the manner of *A Fable for Critics*, with the chief American poets of the time. In another stanza Poe's fondness for analysis and his habit of re-marketing his wares are held up to ridicule.

John R. Thompson, in his lecture on Poe (written apparently at some time in 1860, but not published until 1929), also dwelt on Poe's severity as a critic. See his lecture *The Genius and Character of Edgar Allan Poe*, ed. J. H. Whitty and James H. Rindfleisch, Richmond, 1929, p. 8.

The articles published shortly after Poe's death also made much of his defects as critic. The trait now most stressed was not his causticity, I think, but his disposition to allow his prejudices and personal likes and dislikes to color his critical judgments. Among the first to make this complaint against him was his early friend, John Neal.[1] Griswold declared in his "Memoir" that "his unsupported assertions and opinions were so apt to be influenced by friendship or enmity, by the desire to please or the fear to offend . . . that they should be received in all cases with distrust of their fairness,"[2] an opinion which was echoed by Clark in the *Knickerbocker* for October, 1850.[3] Even Graham admitted that Poe's "outcry" against Longfellow was prejudiced and unjust.[4] A contributor to the *North American Review*[5] expressed the opinion that Poe was intensely prejudiced "against all literature emanating from New England." Evert A. Duyckinck, in 1850, publicly lodged the charge of venality against Poe, declaring that he "was, in the very centre of his soul, a literary attorney, and pleaded according to his fee."[6] Mrs. Gove-Nichols, also, in her novel, *Mary Lyndon*,[7] while apologizing for the poet's weaknesses, admit-

[1] In a letter to Mrs. Mary Gove-Nichols, November 30, 1846, now among the Griswold Papers in the Boston Public Library.

[2] *Poe's Works*, ed. Griswold, III, xlix.

[3] XXXVI, 372.

[4] *Graham's Magazine*, XLIV, 222 (February, 1854).

[5] October, 1856 (LXXXIII, 442).

[6] The *Literary World*, September 21, 1850.

[7] P. 340.

ted that he "sometimes sold favorable opinions, that were not opinions, but shams"; and Clark, in the *Knickerbocker*,[1] characterized him sneeringly as a "jaded hack who runs a broken pace for common hire." Others complained of the over-minuteness of his criticisms and, in particular of his fondness for "verbal fault-finding."[2]

Among those who wrote in praise of his work as a critic were Lowell, Horace Greeley, and Richard Henry Stoddard. Lowell in his sketch of Poe in 1845 declared that he was "at once the most discriminating, philosophical, and fearless critic upon imaginative works . . . in America."[3] Greeley, after hearing his lecture on the American poets in February, 1845, praised him, in the columns of the *Tribune*, dwelling upon his candor and his acuteness, and pronouncing him a "critic of genius and established reputation."[4] Stoddard declared in 1853, "No other modern, save Tennyson, [was] so versed in the philosophy of criticism."[5] Willis praised him enthusiastically in the *Mirror* in 1845 and again in the *Home Journal* at the time of his death.[6]

[1] xxviii, 368 (October, 1846).
[2] See, for instance, Griswold in the New York *Tribune*, October 9, 1849.
[3] *Graham's Magazine*, xxvii, 49.
[4] New York *Tribune*, March 1, 1845.
[5] The *National Magazine*, ii, 198–199.
[6] The *Weekly Mirror*, February 15 and March 8, 1845; the *Home Journal*, October 20, 1849. — John M. Daniel, in the *Southern Literary Messenger*, xvi, 183, while condemning his poems save for "The Raven," wrote: "As a critic we prefer what remains of Edgar Poe to anything after Hazlitt."

V

It appears, then, that the tradition that Poe was neglected by his contemporaries is both true and false. That no one in his time believed him the genius that he is now generally reckoned to be is fairly evident. It is plain, too, that he was not esteemed in his lifetime at his true worth as a poet, although there was one transcendent year — that of the publication of "The Raven" (1845) — during which he was widely praised. But it is also clear that he early came to be favorably known as editor and critic; it is probable, indeed, that his gifts as critic were more widely recognized during his lifetime than they are to-day. And as a writer of tales, although he was slower in gaining recognition in America, it seems clear that he achieved fairly widespread recognition at home before he was thirty-five. That he did not win a larger following among his contemporaries is traceable to various causes, not the least among which was his own personal conduct, — in particular, his weakness for drink, — which many Americans found it impossible to ignore when they came to pass judgment on his accomplishments as a writer. Abroad his reputation began to develop with the publication in 1850 of Griswold's first three volumes of his writings, and his vogue was heightened by the impression which early became current in Europe that he had been unfairly dealt with by his own people.

THE POE–GRISWOLD
CONTROVERSY[1]

I

THE bitterest of all the controversies that have been
waged about Poe is that which grew out of the publication, shortly after his death, of two papers by
Rufus Wilmot Griswold, the poet's literary executor.
These papers — one, an obituary notice that appeared in the New York *Tribune* of October 9, 1849;
the other, Griswold's memoir of Poe, first published
in his edition of Poe's works in September, 1850 —
were both severely condemnatory of the dead poet,
and most of Poe's biographers have held them to be
cruelly unjust; but there have been some — and
among them critics that may speak with the highest
authority — who have pronounced Griswold's judgments upon Poe to be essentially just and fair. I
shall here attempt a fresh examination of the case,
relying mainly on the evidence collected by Poe's
biographers, but taking account also of a number of
documents, mainly from the periodicals of Griswold's
time, that have ordinarily been either overlooked or
ignored.

[1] Reprinted, with revisions and additions, from the *Publications of
the Modern Language Association of America*, xxxiv, 436 f. (September,
1919).

II

Poe and Griswold first met in March, 1841.[1] At that time Poe was editor of *Graham's Magazine*, while Griswold was busily at work on the first of his anthologies, the *Poets and Poetry of America*. Poe's earliest public mention of Griswold appears to have been a brief notice in his "Autography" (published in *Graham's* for December, 1841).[2] He there describes Griswold as "a gentleman of fine taste and sound judgment" and as possessing a "knowledge of American literature, in all its details, [such as] is not exceeded by that of any man among us." Griswold's first public mention of Poe appears to have been the sketch of him printed in the *Poets and Poetry of America* in the spring of 1842. In this sketch Griswold is silent as to Poe's character, but he declares his verses to be "highly imaginative" and "eminently distinguished for their spirituality and skilful versification." [3] During the summer of 1842 Poe wrote for the Boston *Miscellany* a review of Griswold's book in which he reaffirmed his faith in Griswold as a critic and pronounced his anthology "the most important addition which our literature has

[1] Griswold's edition of Poe's Works, I, xxi. My references are to the edition of 1856.

[2] *Poe's Works*, xv, 215.

[3] At the same time, however, he limits the number of Poe's poems that he includes in his anthology to three, although he had made room for twenty-five of Percival's poems and no fewer than thirty-three of Charles Fenno Hoffman's.

for many years received"; [1] and in a letter to Griswold, written about the same time, he assures him that his anthology, though not without faults, was "a better book than any other man in the United States could have made of the materials." [2]

Early in the summer of 1842, Griswold succeeded to the place that Poe had lately vacated as editor of *Graham's Magazine*, and shortly thereafter a coolness sprang up between them. On July 6, 1842, Poe wrote to a Southern correspondent that he intended, in a magazine that he was projecting, to "make war to the knife against the New England assumption of 'All the decency and all the talent' which has been so disgustingly manifested in the Rev. Rufus W. Griswold's 'Poets and Poetry of America.'" [3] He abused Griswold, also, in other letters of this period; [4] and in delivering a lecture on the "Poetry of America" at Philadelphia in November, 1843, and again in Baltimore in January, 1844, he is said to have been "witheringly severe" on Griswold.[5] In the *New World* of March 11, 1843, moreover, there appeared an anonymously written article which has been plausibly attributed to Poe,[6] in which the charge is

[1] See the Boston *Miscellany* for November, 1842, and *Poe's Works*, XI, 156. There was also a brief review in *Graham's Magazine* for June, 1842, which was probably written by Poe.

[2] Griswold, I, xxi.

[3] The *Critic*, April 16, 1892.

[4] Woodberry's *Life of Poe*, I, 353; II, 87.

[5] *Modern Language Notes*, XXVIII, 68 (March, 1913).

[6] Not included among Poe's works by any of his editors, but assigned to him by W. M. Griswold in *Passages from the Correspondence of Rufus*

made that Griswold is "wholly unfit, either by intellect or character, to occupy the editorial chair of *Graham*." [1] Poe made slighting references to Griswold, also, in two articles in the *Columbia Spy* in the summer of 1844,[2] and, likewise in 1844, in the opening paragraph of his story "The Angel of the Odd" (October, 1844). Griswold, on his part, although Poe had condescended on June 11, 1843,[3] to appeal to him for a loan of five dollars on the plea of his wife's illness, circulated about this time or a little later (according to Lowell's friend, C. F. Briggs) some "shocking bad stories" about Poe; [4] and Poe mentions in one of his letters (written "early in 1849") a "beastly article" at his expense, published apparently in 1843, which he suspected Griswold of having written.[5] There followed a period of a year or more when the two were not on speaking terms.

W. Griswold, Cambridge, 1898, p. 118, and apparently also by L. G. Clark in the *Knickerbocker*, xxi, 380 (April, 1843). See below, p. 227, for a discussion of its claims to authenticity.

[1] There also appeared in the Philadelphia *Saturday Museum* early in 1843 an anonymously written review of Griswold's anthology which has been variously ascribed to Poe, in which Griswold is severely attacked and mercilessly ridiculed, his book being characterized as "a very muttonish production" and the editor as "one of the most clumsy of literary thieves" and as knowing no more about poetry than "a Kickapoo Indian." This article is given to Poe by W. F. Gill, who reprints it in his *Life of Poe* (pp. 327–346), by Woodberry (II, 48), and by Harrison (who includes it in his edition of *Poe's Works*, XI, 220–243); but while possibly the work of Poe, the article, as I try to show below (p. 226), was probably the work of some imitator and admirer of the poet.

[2] June 29 and July 6, 1844: see *Doings of Gotham*, ed. Spannuth and Mabbott, pp. 68–69, 76.　　　　[3] Griswold, I, xxi.

[4] Letter of Briggs to Lowell, quoted by Woodberry, II, 123.

[5] Griswold, I, xxii.

But early in 1845 Poe made an attempt to patch up his quarrel with Griswold, writing him a conciliatory letter on January 16, 1845, and asking him for an opportunity to talk over their differences;[1] and they soon resumed, ostensibly at least, their former amicable relations. On repeating his lecture in New York in February, 1845, Poe omitted, as he took pains to assure Griswold, all that might have been objectionable to him;[2] and during the course of the year he published in the *Broadway Journal* two brief notices in which he praised Griswold and his editorial accomplishments.[3] Griswold in turn published during the year an article in which he praised Poe ungrudgingly. This article, which appeared in the Washington *National Intelligencer* of August 30, 1845, is devoted to a consideration of the chief "Tale writers" of America. Charles Brockden Brown, Hawthorne, Cooper, Irving, Willis, and Simms are treated in turn, but Poe is given ampler space and larger praise than any of the rest. "He belongs to the first class of tale writers," says Griswold, and his stories not only possess "a great deal of imagination and fancy," but are "the results of consummate art." In October of the same year Griswold generously responded to an appeal from Poe for a loan of fifty

[1] See Griswold, I, xxii; *Poe's Works*, XVII, 196, 198.
[2] Griswold, I, xxii; *Poe's Works*, XVII, 203.
[3] In his review of "The Magazines" in the *Broadway Journal* of May 17, 1845 (in a note on Hoffman's sketch of Griswold in *Graham's Magazine* for June, 1845), and in his notice of Griswold's edition of *The Prose Works of John Milton* in the *Broadway Journal* for September 27, 1845 (reprinted in *Poe's Works*, XII, 244-247).

dollars to tide over a crisis in the affairs of the *Broadway Journal*.[1] In his *Prose Writers of America*, moreover, — a second famous anthology, compiled largely in 1845,[2] -- he made room for "The Fall of the House of Usher" in its entirety, prefacing it with a sketch of the poet in which he praised both his poems and his tales.[3]

Poe, it seems, published in 1847 a letter relating in some way to Griswold, — a notice of the *Prose Writers*, perhaps, — referred to in one of his letters to Griswold as "Letter in Int., 1847";[4] but this I have been unable to find. It is clear, nevertheless,— whatever may have been the nature of this article,— that another rupture, or partial rupture, between the two had come about in 1846.[5] Their correspondence lapsed during the years 1846–1848; and Mrs. Clemm remarks, in a notice prefixed to the first volume of the Griswold edition of Poe, that their "personal relations" prior to 1849 had "for [some] years been

[1] See Poe's letters of October 26 and November 1, 1845; Griswold, I, xxii.

[2] Not published till the spring of 1847.

[3] He mildly condemns Poe's work as a critic, however; and in later editions he was less liberal in his praise of the tales.

[4] Griswold, I, xxii. "Int." is perhaps an abbreviation for *Intelligencer*, but a fairly careful hunt through the columns of the *National Intelligencer* for 1847 reveals nothing that I can recognize as Poe's.

[5] Or, possibly, late in 1845: see Poe's animadversions on Griswold's poetical anthology in the *Broadway Journal* of November 29, 1845 (*Poe's Works*, XIII, 16), in the course of which he speaks of Griswold as a "dexterous quack." Evidently this breach did not extend to a complete severance of relations; see *Griswold's Correspondence* (p. 230) for mention of a meeting in 1847; and Griswold's "Memoir" (p. xlii) for a meeting in 1848.

interrupted." [1] Griswold is said to have indulged during these years in something of backbiting at Poe's expense; [2] and he further aroused the ill-will of Poe by publishing at some time in 1846, in the *New England Weekly Gazette*, an article in which he drew attention to certain alleged flaws in "The Raven." [3]

A reconciliation between the two again took place, however, with the beginning of the year 1849. Poe in February published in the *Southern Literary Messenger* a favorable notice of Griswold's *Female Poets of America*. [4] Griswold, in turn, on bringing out a new edition of *The Poets and Poetry of America*, enlarged the number of Poe's poems there collected to fourteen. And in June their friendly relations had been so far resumed that Poe felt at liberty to call on Griswold for aid in disposing of certain of his literary wares. [5] On October 7, 1849, Poe died, and it developed soon afterwards that he had expressed the wish shortly before his death that Griswold should serve as his literary executor. On the second day after Poe's death Griswold published in the New York *Tribune* (evening edition) the obituary notice of Poe already referred to as the "Ludwig Article," and in

[1] Griswold, I, iii.

[2] See, in this connection, Sartain, *Reminiscences of a Very Old Man*, New York, 1900, p. 215.

[3] This article I have not seen, nor do I know precisely at what date it appeared; but something of its nature we may glean from a letter of Poe's of December 15, 1846 (see James Southall Wilson, "The Letters of Edgar A. Poe to George W. Eveleth," the *University of Virginia Alumni Bulletin*, XVII, 41 f. [January, 1924]).

[4] Griswold, III, 289–292.   [5] *Ibid.*, I, xxiii.

September of the following year he published his "Memoir" of Poe.

The "Ludwig Article" — Griswold's obituary sketch of Poe [1] — opens with the following paragraph:

EDGAR ALLAN POE IS DEAD. He died in Baltimore the day before yesterday. This announcement will startle many, but few will be grieved by it. The poet was known, personally or by reputation, in all this country; he had readers in England, and in several of the states of Continental Europe; but he had few or no friends; and the regrets for his death will be suggested principally by the consideration that in him literary art lost one of its most brilliant but erratic stars.

Griswold then gives a brief account of Poe's life based largely on the sketch already published in his *Poets and Poetry of America*; after which he enters into an analysis of Poe's mind and character, making therein the following observations derogatory to the poet:

(1) That in character Poe was unamiable, arrogant, irascible, envious, a cynic, and a misanthrope.

(2) That "you could not contradict him but you raised quick choler; you could not speak of wealth, but his cheek paled with gnawing envy."

(3) That "there seemed to him [I quote Griswold's words] no moral susceptibility; and . . . little or nothing of the true point of honor."

[1] Reprinted in *Poe's Works*, I, 348–359.

(4) That he "had, to a morbid excess, that desire to rise which is vulgarly called ambition, but no wish for the esteem or the love of his species; only the hard wish to exceed . . . that he might have the right to despise a world which galled his self-conceit."

The animus behind Griswold's sketch is obvious. As was inevitable, this article called forth a number of protests. N. P. Willis came promptly to the poet's defense in an article in the *Home Journal* of October 20, 1849,[1] in which he expressed vigorous dissent from Griswold's judgment, and suggested that the poet's alleged irregularities of conduct — of which Willis professed to have no first-hand knowledge [2] — were attributable to a "reversed [side of his] character" displayed by him only when he was under the influence of drink. There was also a protest by Henry B. Hirst in the Philadelphia *Saturday Courier* of the same date, in which Griswold's sketch was pronounced "brilliant," but unjust. Three weeks later (on November 13) there appeared in the New York *Tribune* a verse-tribute to the poet's memory, by an anonymous contributor from Chicago, in which Griswold's statement that Poe died friendless was warmly challenged. The attack was continued in the early months of the following year (1850) with the publication (in January) of the first two volumes

[1] *Poe's Works*, I, 360–367.

[2] It should be noted, however, that this testimony conflicts with the testimony given by Willis in an earlier notice of Poe (the *Home Journal*, December 19, 1846), in which he tells of having seen Poe on one occasion when the poet was suffering from the effects of drink.

of Griswold's edition of Poe (the first volume of which included Willis's article, into which the "Ludwig Article" had been incorporated in part). The most spirited of the protests now published was that of George R. Graham,[1] proprietor of the magazine which bore his name and which Poe and Griswold had successively edited. Graham denounced Griswold's sketch as "unfair and untrue," "a fancy sketch of a perverted, jaundiced vision," "an ill-judged and misplaced calumny upon [a] gifted son of genius." Griswold was hotly assailed also by John Neal, in an article published in the Portland *Advertiser* on April 26, 1850. And a defense of the poet, more temperate in tone, was made by the editor of the *American Whig Review*,[2] G. W. Peck, who based his dissent from Griswold on an examination of Poe's writings, and who concluded on this basis that Poe "had as much heart as other men," that he was "a pure-minded gentleman," and that there was no ground for believing that he was "mainly destitute of moral and religious principle."

But there were also those who sided with Griswold. Lewis Gaylord Clark published in the *Knickerbocker* for February, 1850,[3] a notice of Griswold's first two volumes in which he endorsed both Griswold and his appraisal of Poe; and William Wallace is said to have written a reply to Neal's attack on Griswold.[4]

[1] In *Graham's Magazine*, XXXVI, 224-226 (March, 1850).
[2] XI, 301-315 (March, 1850).
[3] XXXV, 163-164.   [4] See Woodberry, II, 452-453.

Others, without specifically mentioning Griswold or writing avowedly in his defense, advanced much the same view as Griswold of Poe's temper and character. C. F. Briggs, Lowell's friend, published an editorial article in *Holden's Dollar Magazine* for December, 1849,[1] in which he describes Poe as "a strange and fearful being," and declares that it would be a bold biographer who would dare to make such a revelation of his life as the task demanded. George Ripley, in reviewing these volumes in the *Tribune* of January 17, 1850, remarked that Poe was a man of "uncommon genius," but that he "had no earnestness of character, no sincerity of conviction, no faith in human excellence"; and John M. Daniel, a fire-eating editor of Richmond, contributed an article to the *Southern Literary Messenger* of March, 1850,[2] in which, while condemning Griswold, he went even farther than Griswold or his defenders in condemnation of Poe.[3]

These articles made it clear that Poe had a number of bitter enemies; but they also served to show that he was not without loyal friends, and they tended to

[1] IV, 765–766. The article was unsigned, but was evidently by Briggs, who was editor of the magazine.

[2] XVI, 172–187.

[3] It is only fair to Poe to say that three of these five — Briggs, Clark, and Daniel — nursed a grudge of some sort against him. Briggs and Poe had quarrelled in 1845 over the *Broadway Journal*, and Briggs had been attacked by Poe in the *Literati* papers (*Poe's Works*, xv, 20–23); Clark, also, had been "used up" by Poe in the *Literati* papers (*ibid.*, pp. 114–116); and Daniel had been challenged by Poe to fight a duel in the summer of 1848 (Woodberry, II, 273, 443 ff.; Whitty, *The Complete Poems of Poe*, p. lxix).

discredit, in a measure, Griswold's statements as to the perversity of his character.

III

Griswold's "Memoir" of Poe was first published in 1850 as a part of the third volume of the Griswold edition of Poe's works, in which it comprises some thirty pages.[1] It is introduced by a note from Griswold in which he endeavors to justify his course in publishing the "Ludwig Article" on the ground that at the time he was unaware of his appointment as Poe's executor; and he intimates that he had felt impelled to write the article by the attacks that had been made upon him by Graham and Neal.

It may be noted, however, in passing, that although there is nothing to show that Poe, in selecting Griswold as his executor, intended that he should also serve as his biographer, — Mrs. Clemm's statement (in a notice "To the Reader" prefixed to the first volume of the Griswold edition) is fairly explicit to the effect that it was the poet's desire merely that Griswold should act as literary executor and "superin-

[1] It first appeared about the middle of September, 1850; see the New York *Tribune* for September 14, 1850, and the *Literary World* for September 21, 1850. It was also published about the same time in the *International Monthly Magazine* (for October, 1850); see the New York *Tribune* of September 25 and the *Literary World* of September 28, 1850.

The "Memoir," though first published in the third volume of Griswold's edition, was transferred to the first volume on the publication of a second edition in 1853, and it continued to occupy this position on the publication of an edition of four volumes in 1856.

tend the publications of his works," [1] while Willis was looked to for "observations upon his life and character," — Griswold's statement in a letter of October 31, 1849, to Lowell, makes it clear that he already had in mind at that time the publication of his "Memoir." [2] He here speaks of "giving notice perhaps [in the advertisement to the first volumes published] of an intention to prepare his life and correspondence hereafter." And there is evidence from a different source that he had already set about collecting material for a memoir before the end of the year. This evidence is afforded by a letter of John R. Thompson's to Griswold, written December 21, 1849, in which the following sentence occurs: "I have too long delayed sending you the promised mems of poor Poe, and I fear that what I now enclose will be of little value, scarcely sufficient to warrant their incorporation into the Life." [3] That he was further actuated in the writing of the "Memoir" by the attacks made upon him by Graham and others there is no reason to doubt. [4]

In the "Memoir" Griswold enters much more fully into a consideration of Poe's writings than he had

[1] Griswold, also, in a note prefixed to the "Memoir" interprets his office to be simply "the collection of his works and their publication."

[2] This letter is preserved among the Lowell Manuscripts in the Harvard College Library.

[3] This letter is preserved among the Griswold Papers in the Boston Public Library. See also a letter of Griswold to John Pendleton Kennedy (the *Sewanee Review*, xxv, 198 [April, 1917]).

[4] See in this connection a letter to J. T. Fields (of September 25, 1850), published in *Passages from the Correspondence of Griswold*, p. 267.

done in the obituary sketch, and he also develops at greater length the details of Poe's life. His judgments on Poe's writings are, for the most part, commendatory, and coincide, in the main, with the view now generally held. In his observations on Poe's life and character, however, he is much more severe than he had been in the *Tribune* article. The old charges of arrogance, envy, misanthropy, and a debased sense of honor reappear, and the following additional charges are brought forward:

(1) That while a student at the University of Virginia Poe had "led a very dissipated life," and that he had been expelled in consequence of his excesses there.[1]

(2) That after leaving West Point he had enlisted in the United States Army, but had presumably deserted.[2]

(3) That he had been guilty of a still darker crime in his relations with the second Mrs. Allan.[3]

(4) That in certain of his publications — among them his *Conchologist's First Book* — he had been guilty of plagiarisms that were "scarcely paralleled for their audacity in all literary history." [4]

(5) That his "unsupported assertions and opinions were so apt to be influenced by friendship or enmity . . . that they should be received in all cases with distrust of their fairness." [5]

(6) That he exhibited "scarcely any virtue in

[1] Griswold, I, xxv–xxvi.   [2] *Ibid.*, p. xxvii.   [3] *Ibid.*
[4] *Ibid.*, p. xlviii.   [5] *Ibid.*, p. xlix.

either his life or his writings," and that both his life and his writings were "without a recognition or a manifestation of conscience." [1]

He closes by repeating from the "Ludwig Article" the following passage:

> There seemed to him no moral susceptibility; and, what was more remarkable in a proud nature, little or nothing of the true point of honor. He had, to a morbid excess, that desire to rise which is vulgarly called ambition, but no wish for the esteem or the love of his species; only the hard wish to succeed — not shine, not serve — succeed, that he might have the right to despise a world which galled his self-conceit.

This sketch, coming as it did from the approved editor of Poe and presented with much circumstantiality, had the effect of silencing for a time most of Poe's defenders. It was adopted as authentic in all save a very few of the contemporary notices of Griswold's edition of Poe's works, and in virtually every other edition of Poe's writings that appeared during the first two decades after the poet's death. Among reviews in which it is accepted as authentic (or largely so) are those published in the Richmond *Whig* for September 28, 1850; the *Knickerbocker* for October, 1850; the *Democratic Review* for December, 1850, and January and February, 1851; the *Westminster Review* for January, 1852; *Tait's Magazine* for April, 1852; [2] *Chambers's Edinburgh*

---

[1] *Ibid.*, p. xlvii.
[2] Reprinted in *Littell's Living Age*, XXXIII, 422-424.

Journal for February 26, 1853; [1] Gilfillan's *Third Gallery of Portraits*, 1854; [2] the *North American Review* for October, 1856; *Fraser's Magazine* for June, 1857; and the *Edinburgh Review* for April, 1858.

The writer of the first of these reviews, John R. Thompson, [3] editor of the *Southern Literary Messenger*, took occasion in commenting on Griswold's "Memoir" to say that it was, in his judgment, "truthful," and that such "hard things" as Griswold had brought out seemed "to have been brought out because their suppression would have been as palpable a departure from an honest estimate of the poet, as a direct misstatement of any of his qualities." Lewis Gaylord Clark, editor of the *Knickerbocker*, who had, in February, 1850, vouched for the correctness of the "Ludwig Article," also made occasion to vouch for the correctness of this second article of Griswold's. [4] There were those, too, who went farther than Griswold had gone. The writer of the notice in the *Edinburgh Review*, [5] for instance, declared that Poe was "a blackguard of undeniable mark" and that "the lowest abyss of moral imbecility and disrepute" had never been attained until Poe's

[1] *Littell's Living Age*, XXXVII, 157–161.

[2] Pp. 374 ff. First published in the London *Critic*, and reprinted in the *Southern Literary Messenger*, XX, 249 f. (April, 1854), and in *Littell's Living Age*, XLI, 166–171.

[3] That this review was from the pen of Thompson is established by a letter of Thompson's, of September 30, 1850, to Griswold; now among the Griswold Papers in the Boston Public Library.

[4] See the *Knickerbocker*, XXXVI, 370–372 (October, 1850).

[5] CVII, 420–421 (April, 1858).

advent into this world; while the reviewer in the London *Critic*, George Gilfillan, a British clergyman, boldly asserted that Poe's "heart was as rotten as his conduct was infamous," that he had "absolutely no virtue or good quality," and that he broke his wife's heart, "hurrying her to a premature grave, that he might write 'Annabel Lee' and 'The Raven.'" [1]

Of outspoken public protests at this time there were amazingly few. The only vigorous protest that was promptly forthcoming, so far as I am aware, was that of an anonymous contributor to the *Saturday Evening Post* of September 21, 1850. This reviewer (probably the editor of the *Post*, Henry Peterson), while admitting that he held "no very exalted opinion of Mr. Poe's character," insisted, nevertheless, that he was unable to find any excuse for Griswold's course; and he suggests that Griswold perhaps understood *literary executor* to mean "one who executes." Continuing, he says:

Considering this biography as the work of a literary executor, we must say that a more cold-blooded and ungenerous composition has seldom come under our notice. Nothing so condemnatory of Mr. Poe, so absolutely blasting to his character has ever appeared in print. . . . It is absolutely horrible (considering the circumstances under which Mr. Griswold writes) with what cool deliberateness he charges upon Mr. Poe the basest and most dishonorable actions.

[1] *A Third Gallery of Portraits*, London, 1854, p. 376. Another clergyman, A. K. H. Boyd (*Critical Essays of a Country Parson*, London, 1867, p. 248), is perhaps echoing this statement of Gilfillan's when he asserts that Poe "starved his wife, and broke her heart."

Others, while not excepting to the facts as set down by Griswold, demurred to the spirit of his article. The reviewer in *Fraser's Magazine*,[1] for instance, Rev. A. K. H. Boyd, remarked that it was "curious . . . how little pains the biographer takes to conceal the shortcomings of his hero"; and the editor of the *Democratic Review*[2] pleads with the critics of Poe not to "rattle his bones." E. A. Duyckinck, editor of the *Literary World*,[3] while apparently accepting Griswold's account of Poe's life, inquired whether Griswold in republishing the *Literati* papers had not tampered with his text, and drew attention to the fact that Griswold was careful to omit "any unhandsome references" to himself.

Graham is said to have written Mrs. Clemm in the fall of 1850 that he and other friends were determined to come to Poe's defense;[4] but in the December number of his magazine he dismissed the matter with the statement that "by the decision of several discreet friends of the lamented Poe" he was omitting "a number of letters and articles which [had] been collected in relation to his life and writings," giving as his reason that "the wounds made by his criticisms are too fresh — the conflicting interests too many, to hope now to do that justice which time and the sober second thought of educated minds will accord to his memory"; and he concludes with the

[1] LV, 684–700 (June, 1857). Also in *Critical Essays of a Country Parson*, London, 1867, pp. 210–248.   [2] XXVIII, 172 (February, 1851).
[3] VII, 228–229 (September 21, 1850).
[4] Ingram's *Life and Letters of Poe*, p. 432.

promise (made good in *Graham's* for February, 1854) to perform at some later time "the grateful duty" which he felt himself to owe to the poet.[1] Willis republished in his *Hurrygraphs* in 1851 his reply to the "Ludwig Article"; and in an editorial in the *Home Journal* in 1856 [2] he branded the article published in the *North American Review* in the same year (in which some of the severest of Griswold's charges had been rehashed) as "uncharitable," "needlessly severe," and, in some of its conclusions, "merciless." He also republished in the *Home Journal* of March 16, 1850, Graham's first article on Poe, declaring at the same time that it was "most creditable to Graham"; and he admitted to the columns of the *Home Journal* (March 30, 1850) a stinging reply to Daniel's article in the *Messenger*. Significant, too, is a letter of his to George P. Morris written in October, 1859 (quoted by Ingram[3]), in which he remarks (p. xlviii): "You remember how absolutely and how good-humoredly ready he was for any suggestion; how punctually and industriously reliable in the following out of the wish once expressed; how cheerful and present-minded his work when he might excusably have been so listless and abstracted"; and adds: "We loved the man for the entireness of the fidelity with which he served us."

As time passed, the number of those who were

---

[1] *Graham's Magazine*, xxxvii, 390 (December, 1850).
[2] October 18, 1856.
[3] In his edition of *Poe's Works*, 1874, i, xlvii–xlviii.

unwilling to accept Griswold's account steadily increased. In February, 1852, C. C. Burr, who had known Poe in his darkest days, contributed to the *Nineteenth Century* [1] a brief article in which he dissented from Griswold's imputation to Poe of ingratitude and heartlessness. "He was," writes Burr, "in the core of his heart, a grateful, single-minded, loving kind of man . . . a very gentle, thoughtful, scrupulously refined, and modest kind of man," who although "he had faults and many weaknesses," had also "a congregation of virtues which made him *loved* as well as admired by those who knew him best." Stoddard, although evidently antagonistical to Poe at heart, admitted, in an article in the *National Magazine* for March, 1853,[2] that the biographical sketches of Poe had been written "by indifferent friends or open foes," and that they had been "needlessly cruel." In August, 1853, an anonymous contributor to the *Waverley Magazine*, in speaking of the inaccuracy of Griswold's "Memoir," expressed the hope that it would not be long before an "unbiased life and collection of Poe's works" should be published. In the following year Graham published his second article in defense of Poe, in which he again protested against the accusations of looseness in money matters and of habitual unfairness in his criticisms.[3] Two years later appeared Baudelaire's

---

[1] v, 19–33.   [2] ii, 197.

[3] See *Graham's Magazine*, xliv, 216–225 (February, 1854). He further declares that Poe was a "long-suffering, much-persecuted, greatly-belied man [who] had a soul as soft, as delicate, as tender as a child's," and that

famous sketch of Poe,[1] in which a vehement protest
was made against the tone and spirit of Griswold's
account. The next year (1857) a lively defense of
Poe by J. Wood Davidson appeared in *Russell's
Magazine*.[2] In the same year, L. A. Godey, editor of
Godey's Lady's Book, wrote to the editor of the
Knickerbocker[3] to say that he was not to be "counted
in among those . . . to whom . . . Poe proved faith-
less," and that the poet's conduct toward him was
"in all respects honorable and unblameworthy." In
1859, another Philadelphia acquaintance of Poe's,
L. A. Wilmer, in his book, *Our Press Gang*, remon-
strated against Griswold's treatment of Poe.[4] And
toward the end of the year 1859 appeared Mrs. Whitman's *Edgar Poe and his Critics*, an entire volume
devoted to the defense of Poe and directed mainly
against Griswold, whose "Memoir" of Poe she declares to be unjust and misleading and to involve
"remorseless violations of the trust confided to him."[5]

"every effervescence of excess, of anger, of irritation, or of wrong done
to others, was followed by an agony of penitence, and oftentimes by
earnest, long-sustained and half-successful efforts at reformation." He
explains the attacks upon Poe after his death as dictated largely by a
spirit of revenge on the part of those whom he had antagonized by his
criticisms and reviews. But he admits that Poe's criticisms were in some
cases unjust; and he instances his attacks upon Longfellow as among the
few that were "utterly unjust."

  [1] "Edgar Poe: sa vie et ses œuvres"; published as an introduction to
his translation of Poe's tales.
  [2] II, 171 (November, 1857).
  [3] XLIX, 106 (January, 1857).
  [4] See especially pp. 284–285. See also a more detailed defense of Poe
by Wilmer in the Baltimore *Daily Commercial*, May 23, 1866.
  [5] Pp. 11, 14, 15.

Among other articles in defense of Poe that appeared during the next decade are articles by Mayne Reid,[1] who had known the Poes in Philadelphia, and Thomas Cottrell Clarke, a Philadelphia printer and publisher who had known him intimately.[2] There appeared also, in 1866, a strange article by one who styles himself Parke Van Parke [3] and who professes to write at the instance of the poet's sister, Rosalie Poe, in which Griswold's memoir is pronounced the most "atrocious instance of human iniquity . . . since the days of Cain."

IV

Such was the contemporary attitude to Griswold's "Memoir" of Poe. What, now, does an examination of Griswold's sketch in the light of our maturer knowledge of Poe as brought out by his editors and biographers reveal as to the trustworthiness of Griswold's account? Such an inquiry reveals, first of all, that some of the ugliest charges made by Griswold against Poe were based on Poe's own misstatements to Griswold. The authority for the charge that Poe led, while at the University of Virginia, a "very dissipated life" [4] turns out to be a document in Poe's handwriting sent to Griswold in March, 1841,[5] and now preserved in the Poe Shrine at Richmond.

[1] *Onward*, I, 305–308 (April, 1869).
[2] The *Newark Northern Monthly*, II, 234 f. (January, 1868).
[3] See his *Discussions and Diversions*, Philadelphia, 1866, p. 264.
[4] Griswold, I, xxv.
[5] *Poe's Works*, I, 344–346.

Chargeable to Poe also are Griswold's inaccuracies as to the date of Poe's birth,[1] as to the duration of his stay in London when a boy,[2] and as to an alleged second expedition to Europe in 1827.[3] Investigation has also shown that Griswold was correct in charging that Poe had made questionable use of another's materials in the composition of his *Conchologist's First Book*.[4] And it is now reasonably clear that Poe was sometimes actuated by considerations of self-interest or by a feeling of jealousy in his critical judgments.

But there is a good deal of error in Griswold's "Memoir" for which we can be certain that Poe was not responsible. It has long since been established that Poe was not expelled from the University of Virginia. Nor is there any reason to believe that he ever deserted from the army. And the sole basis for the vile insinuation of an attempted assault upon the person of Mrs. Allan is the quite unsupported assertion of John M. Daniel,[5] in whose testimony very little reliance may be placed. That Poe was without friends at the time of his death or that he was in-

[1] Griswold, relying on Poe's autobiographical memorandum, gives the date as 1811.

[2] Griswold had followed Poe in stating that the period of his stay in England was 1816 to 1822; in reality it covered the years 1815 to 1820.

[3] This yarn survives in several different versions, all apparently traceable to Poe. See Woodberry, I, 72 f., 365 f., and the *Sewanee Review*, XX, 209-210 (April, 1912).

[4] See *Poe's Works*, I, 146-148, and Woodberry, I, 194-198. Griswold, however (I, xlviii-xlix), badly overstates the case against Poe as a plagiarist.

[5] The *Southern Literary Messenger*, XVI, 176 (March, 1850).

capable of gratitude for service done has been dis-
proved over and over again by the testimony of
those who knew him best; while the charge that he
was without a sense of honor or without any manifestation of conscience is too sweeping to call for
serious consideration.[1]

Other charges, involving certain contemporaries
of Poe, were specifically denied by those affected,
either publicly or by letter, soon after the appearance
of the "Memoir." Within ten days after the publication of the "Memoir," Longfellow wrote to Griswold to correct his statement that he had "been
shown by Mr. Longfellow . . . a series of papers
which constitute a demonstration that Mr. Poe was
indebted to him for the idea of 'The Haunted Palace.'"[2] In the New York *Tribune* of June 7, 1852,
W. J. Pabodie, a friend of Mrs. Whitman, made
a formal denial of Griswold's charge that Poe had,
at some time in 1848, committed at the home of
Mrs. Whitman "such outrages as made necessary a
summons of the police." Further denials were made
by Mrs. Whitman herself in her book, *Edgar Poe and
his Critics*.[3] A score of years later J. H. B. Latrobe

[1] Among minor inaccuracies in Griswold's account are the allegations
(1) that Poe was not born at Boston (Griswold, I, xxxvii); (2) that "not
a line by Poe was purchased for Graham's Magazine" for "four or five
years" before the poet's death (*ibid.*, p. li: in reality two articles by Poe
appeared in *Graham's* in 1849); and (3) that Poe "prepared with his own
hands" the sketch of his life contributed by H. B. Hirst to the *Saturday
Museum* in February, 1843 (*ibid.*, p. 1).

[2] Griswold, I, xlviii; *Poe's Works*, XVII, 406–408.

[3] Mrs. Whitman (p. 15) speaks also of an article in the *Home Journal*,

corrected some inaccuracies in Griswold's account of the deliberations of the judges on the occasion of the awarding to Poe his first short-story prize in 1833.[1]

It is proper to note also — what the reader can hardly escape noting — that Griswold, although he writes as literary executor, assumes in his comments on Poe as a man an attitude of undisguised hostility. He does, in truth, introduce the gracious testimony of Mrs. Osgood as to Poe's chivalrous conduct toward women and as to his affection for his invalid wife; but he is careful to state that Mrs. Osgood accepted his analysis of Poe's character as accurate and that she meant to testify only as to the character assumed by the poet when in the presence of women.[2] And in justification of his course he argues, forsooth, that "it has always been made a portion of the penalty of wrong that its anatomy should be displayed for the common study and advantage." [3]

The conclusion, then, is inevitable that a number of the harsher things said about Poe by Griswold are true, and that certain inaccuracies in his account rest upon Poe's inaccurate statements to him; but that most of the more damaging things charged against Poe by Griswold are either without substantial basis in fact or are greatly exaggerated; and,

in 1859 or slightly earlier, in which a "calumnious story" proceeding from Griswold was refuted.
[1] Griswold, I, xxviii; *Edgar Allan Poe: A Memorial Volume*, ed. Miss S. S. Rice, Baltimore, 1877, p. 59.
[2] Griswold, I, lii-liv.   [3] *Ibid.*, p. xlvii.

further, that Griswold both discredits himself and discounts his judgments with respect to Poe by consistently assuming, in his comments upon the poet's character, an attitude of unabashed hostility to him.

V

It remains to inquire into the charge that has been made against Griswold of garbling certain of Poe's letters in his effort to strengthen his case against the poet.

In the preface of his "Memoir," Griswold includes eleven letters that he had received from Poe. The originals of only six of these have come down to us.[1] Four of these six originals differ only slightly and immaterially from the versions printed by Griswold; but two of them exhibit startling variations from Griswold's text.[2] To make these discrepancies as graphic as possible, I have reproduced here the two letters as printed by Griswold, putting in italics the more important passages which do not appear in the postmarked originals and enclosing in brackets certain passages that appear in the originals but do not appear in Griswold's text.[3]

[1] Five of these (see *Poe's Works*, xvii, 83–84, 198, 200–201, 202–203, 216) are in the Boston Public Library (four of the number being postmarked originals); and the sixth (*ibid.*, pp. 346–347) — which is unhappily incomplete as preserved — is in the Wrenn Library of the University of Texas.

[2] One of these is printed in *Poe's Works* (xvii, 200–202) with the two versions juxtaposed.

[3] For each of these letters I use Griswold's text as the basis for comparison.

[88]

The first letter, dated February 24, 1845, runs as follows:

My dear Griswold: — *A thousand thanks for your kindness in the matter of those books, which I could not afford to buy, and had so much need of.* Soon after seeing you, I sent you, through Zieber, all my poems worth republishing, and I presume they reached you. *I was sincerely delighted with what you said of them, and if you will write your criticism in the form of a preface, I shall be greatly obliged to you. I say this not because you praised me: everybody praises me now: but because you so perfectly understand me, or what I have aimed at, in all my poems: I did not think you had so much delicacy of appreciation joined with your strong sense; I can say truly that no man's approbation gives me so much pleasure.* I send you with this another package, also through Zieber, by Burgess & Stringer. It contains, in the way of essay, "Mesmeric Revelation," which I would like to have go in, even if you have to omit the "House of Usher." [I send also a portion of the "Marginalia," in which I have marked some of the most pointed passages.] I send also corrected copies of (in the way of funny criticism, but you don't like this) "Flaccus," which conveys a tolerable idea of my style; and of my serious manner "Barnaby Rudge" is a good specimen. [In "Graham" you will find these.] In the tale line, "The Murders of the Rue Morgue," "The Gold Bug," and the "Man that Was Used Up" — far more than enough, but you can select to suit yourself. I prefer the "G. B." to the "M. in the R. M." [but have not a copy just now. If there is no immediate hurry for it, however, I will get one & send it you corrected. Please write & let me know if you get this.] I have taken a third interest in the "Broadway Journal," and will be glad if you could send me anything [at any time, in the way of "Literary Intelligence"] *for it.*

Why not let me anticipate the book publication of your splendid essay on Milton?

Truly yours,

Poe.

The second letter is "without date" (and is so described by Griswold), but the original manuscript as mailed to Griswold bears the postmark "New York Apr. 19," and it is evident, both from Griswold's statement that it was Poe's "next" letter after the letter of February 24,[1] and from the reference to Poe's New York lecture (delivered February 28, 1845), that it was written in 1845.

Dear Griswold: — I return the proofs with many thanks for your attentions. The poems look quite as well in the short metres as in the long *ones*, and I am quite content as it is. [You will perceive, however, that some of the lines have been divided at the wrong place. I have marked them right in the proof; but lest there should be any misapprehension, I copy them as they should be. . . .[2] Near the beginning of the poem you have "nodded" spelt "nooded."] In "The Sleeper" you have "Forever with unclosed eye" for [3] "Forever with unopen'd eye." Is it possible to make the correction? I presume you understand that in the repetition of my Lecture on the Poets, (in N. Y.) I left out *all* that was offensive to yourself.[4] *I am ashamed of myself that I ever said anything of you that was so unfriendly or so*

[1] Griswold, I, xxii.

[2] Here Poe quotes four lines from "The Raven," dividing each line into two lines: see *Poe's Works*, XVII, 202.

[3] The original manuscript has "the line" where Griswold has "you have," and "should read" where Griswold has "for"; and also has the word "alteration" where Griswold has "correction."

[4] This sentence appears as a postscript in the original manuscript.

[90]

unjust; but what I did say I am confident has been misrepresented to you. See my notice of C. F. Hoffman's (?) sketch of you.

Very sincerely yours,

Poe.

How to account for these discrepancies is not at once clear. Possibly Griswold relied upon rejected drafts of the letters, found (on this supposition) by him among Poe's papers, — what we know happened, indeed, in the case of a letter of Poe's of March 10, 1847, to Mrs. Jane E. Locke (the manuscript may still be seen among the Griswold Papers in the Boston Public Library).[1] But obviously appearances are against Griswold, for it is just those passages that are somehow complimentary to him that do not appear in the original manuscripts. And in at least one instance it is evident that Griswold actually interpolated matter that proceeded from his own pen. I refer to the closing sentence in the letter last quoted above: "See my notice of C. F. Hoffman's (?) sketch of you." Poe's letter to Griswold is postmarked "Apr. 19," but Hoffman's sketch of Griswold (or at least the sketch attributed to Hoffman which Griswold represents Poe as referring to) did not appear until some time in May (being a part of the June issue of *Graham's Magazine*), and was noticed by Poe in the *Broadway Journal* for May 17.[2] This sentence,

[1] It is reproduced in *Poe's Works*, xvii, 280 f. See in this connection Griswold, i, xli, and also a letter from Mrs. Jane E. Locke touching the matter in *Griswold's Correspondence*, p. 265.

[2] i, 316.

then, referring as it does to an article which was not in existence at the time that Poe's letter was written and which was not to appear in print till some four weeks after the date of Poe's letter, was plainly forged by Griswold.

Whether or not any of the remaining sentences in question are ungenuine we cannot be certain; but with the establishment of the fact that one of the suspected sentences was the work of Griswold, the presumption is greatly strengthened that all of the suspected sentences proceeded from him. In other words, it would appear that each of the italicized sentences in the letters printed above was forged and interpolated by Griswold.[1] Another passage which in all likelihood proceeded from Griswold is to be found in the words "one of our great little cliquists and claquers" (referring to Evert A. Duyckinck) which appear in Griswold's text[2] of a letter of Poe's, dated August 9, 1846, to P. P. Cooke, but which do not appear in the original manuscript of that letter.[3] It would seem that Griswold also took the liberty of abridging and otherwise altering, in his "Memoir," one of his own letters to Poe: see the text of that letter as printed by Griswold which Professor Harrison, in his edition of Poe's letters,

---

[1] Griswold points out in his "Memoir" (I, li) two instances in which Poe, in quoting from letters received by him, departed slightly from his originals. But Poe's derelictions in this particular will scarcely be held to excuse or to palliate Griswold's.

[2] I, xlvii.   [3] See *Poe's Works*, XVII, 228.

juxtaposes with the text of the original manuscript of that letter.[1]

VI

What, finally, of the integrity of Griswold's editing of Poe? Evert A. Duyckinck in his review of the third volume of the Griswold edition of Poe (printed immediately after the appearance of that volume) [2] raises the question whether the *Literati* papers (first collected there) had not "undergone editorial revisal." Both Ingram [3] and Gill [4] have made a similar imputation of editorial recklessness against Griswold, instancing, in particular, the article on Thomas Dunn English, as bearing the marks of having been tampered with. More recently the editors of the "Virginia Poe" have charged that Griswold not only tampered with the text of the *Literati*, but that he also took indefensible liberties with still other papers. Specifically, it is alleged that Griswold substituted for five of the *Literati* papers (those on Briggs, English, Lawson, Mrs. Osgood, and Mrs. Hewitt) "other papers in the Poe manner," [5] and that in the case of a number of Poe's reviews he made free to combine two or more papers into one, to omit or to transpose numerous passages of considerable length, and to mutilate in still other ways his originals.[6]

Such comparison as I have made of Griswold's

---

[1] *Ibid.*, pp. 197–198.   [2] The *Literary World*, September 21, 1850.
[3] *Poe's Works*, Edinburgh, 1874, i, lxi.
[4] *The Life of Edgar Allan Poe*, p. 179.
[5] *Poe's Works*, xv, ix, 263.   [6] *Ibid.*, x, vi–vii.

text of Poe's writings with their originals leads me to believe — indeed, convinces me — that Griswold, judged by standards of to-day, was not a careful editor. It is reasonably plain that he silently altered the titles of several of Poe's poems and tales.[1] It is all but certain that he did not always adopt Poe's latest text.[2] He allowed numerous typographical errors to escape him.[3] And he omitted from his edition some things of importance that were surely known to him — among them the earlier lyric "To Helen." That he also made bold here and there to prune away matter that he felt to be unimportant, or that he even transposed parts of certain papers and combined others, I think not improbable.[4]

But that Griswold made any very substantial changes in the text of Poe's critical papers or that he introduced any papers not actually written by Poe I doubt very much. The article on Mrs. Osgood as printed by him among the *Literati* papers [5] turns out

[1] By omitting Poe's sub-titles: see, for instance, "Ulalume" and "Hop-Frog." And in at least two instances, as I have pointed out in *Modern Language Notes*, XLII, 519–520 (December, 1927), he indulged in an even more serious tampering with his text, in the substitution in "King Pest" of the word *nature* for Poe's word *nare* (*Poe's Works*, II, 180) and of *saneness* for *sameness* in "Morella" (*ibid.*, p. 29) in a passage that Poe had quoted from Locke.

[2] See the variant readings of "The Raven," "Lenore," and "Dream-Land."

[3] See the list of *errata* collected by the editors of *Poe's Works*, II–VIII, *passim*.

[4] It is altogether probable, for instance, that Griswold was responsible for the combining of the several articles in reply to "Outis" into one article.

[5] Griswold, III, 87–99; reprinted in *Poe's Works*, XV, 271-288.

to be, as Professor Woodberry has already noted,[1] a review of Mrs. Osgood's poems contributed by Poe to the *Southern Literary Messenger* of August, 1849. Another of the *Literati* papers whose authenticity has been questioned, that entitled "Thomas Dunn Brown," [2] survives in a manuscript in Poe's autograph, owned by the Rosenbach Company of Philadelphia.

The three remaining *Literati* papers supposed to have been substituted by Griswold without authority — namely, those on Briggs, Lawson, and Mrs. Hewitt — were, I imagine, either similarly based on manuscripts found by Griswold among Poe's papers (as in the case of the article on English) or had already been published in some periodical (as in the case of the article on Mrs. Osgood). Professor Woodberry suggests [3] that these articles (he includes also the article on English) were a part of a volume variously entitled [4] "The American Parnassus," "A Critical History of American Literature," "Living Writers of America," and "The Authors of America in Prose and Verse," on which Poe was engaged for half a dozen years before his death; and this suggestion is confirmed, so far as the article on English is con-

---

[1] In an unsigned review in the New York *Nation* for December 4, 1902, p. 446. I owe it to Professor Woodberry to say that I have been anticipated by him in still other conclusions reached here and, likewise, in my general conclusions as to Griswold's editing.

[2] Griswold, III, 101–104; *Poe's Works*, xv, 266–270.

[3] The *Nation*, December 4, 1902, p. 446.

[4] Either in Poe's references to it in his letters, or in contemporary advance notices of it in the press.

cerned, by the manuscript containing the "Thomas Dunn Brown" article, which contains also holograph copies of the *Literati* papers on Richard Adams Locke and Christopher Pearse Cranch, and which bears the title "Literary America." [1]

So, also, it seems to me altogether probable that the longer passages believed to be unauthentic in Griswold's texts of Poe's reviews [2] are, in reality, the work of Poe, and that Poe, likewise, was responsible for much, if not most, of the curtailing and rearranging exhibited in Griswold's edition. [3] As is well known,

[1] Now in the possession of the Rosenbach Company, by whose courtesy I am permitted to quote from it. The rest of the title-page of this manuscript, which is dated "1848," runs in part as follows: "Some Honest Opinions about our Autorial Merits and Demerits / with / Occasional Words of Personality. / By Edgar A. Poe."

[2] The chief reviews which exhibit important variations in the Griswold edition are those on Hawthorne (Griswold, III, 188–202; *Poe's Works*, XIII, 142–155, XI, 104–113), the Davidson sisters (Griswold, III, 219–228; *Poe's Works*, X, 174–178, 221–226), R. M. Bird (Griswold, III, 257–261; *Poe's Works*, VIII, 63–73, IX, 137–139), Griswold (Griswold, III, 283–292; *Poe's Works*, XI, 147–160), Longfellow (Griswold, III, 292–334; *Poe's Works*, XII, 41–106), a second paper on Longfellow (Griswold, III, 363–374; *Poe's Works*, XI, 64–85), Mrs. Browning (Griswold, III, 401–424; *Poe's Works*, XII, 1–35), and R. H. Horne (Griswold, III, 425–444; *Poe's Works*, XI, 249–275). By an unhappy oversight, the last six paragraphs of the second of the two papers on the Davidson sisters (as published in *Graham's Magazine* for December, 1841) are omitted in *Poe's Works* (X, 226), thus making Griswold's supposed irregularities in the case of this article appear much more serious than they actually are.

The paper on Mrs. Lewis (Griswold, III, 242–249; *Poe's Works*, XIII, 215–225), for which no place of prior publication has hitherto been pointed out, appeared condensed and freely paraphrased in the sketch of Mrs. Lewis included by Griswold in his anthology of *The Female Poets of America*. The papers on Bayard Taylor and William Wallace, which Griswold prints as separate articles (III, 207–209, 240–241), were printed originally in the "Marginalia" (*Poe's Works*, XVI, 145–148, 175–176).

[3] In the case of the "Marginalia" the order adopted by Griswold is

Poe was constantly revising work that he had already published. Some of the recasting that he may be supposed to have made in his critical articles was made, in all likelihood, with a view to incorporating these articles in his "Literary America," which was to include, not only the writers of New York City (to which the *Literati* papers as published in *Godey's* and the *Democratic Review* had been restricted), but in addition writers of note from all parts of America — in fact, it is described, in one of the titles under which it is referred to, as "A Critical History of American Literature." [1]

But what most inclines me to doubt that Griswold wrote any considerable part of the matter thought to have been interpolated or substituted by him in Poe's essays is the complete lack of motive for such a course.[2] Griswold was a busy man; and there was in the case of these papers — the case was different with Poe's letters — nothing for him to gain by tampering with them: there is in these suspected passages nothing that would tend to exhibit Poe in

so radically different from that originally adopted as to present a veritable puzzle to one who would unravel the mystery of their arrangement. So far as I can discover, no logical system of arrangement has been followed by Griswold. It looks as though the separate items might have been thrown pell-mell into a basket and then taken out at haphazard and published in the order drawn.

[1] See Woodberry, II, 96. In a notice of this projected work, in the Philadelphia *Saturday Courier* of July 25, 1846, moreover, the statement is made that it will "embrace the whole Union"; and a similar statement was made by Hirst in his sketch of Poe in the *Saturday Museum*.

[2] This point has been dwelt on by Professor Woodberry in his article in the *Nation* (December 4, 1902, p. 446).

a darker light, nothing that would in any way inure to Griswold's benefit. And there is, besides, the test of style. Griswold wrote at times with exceptional pungency and vigor; but it is not very difficult to distinguish his manner from Poe's. There is, I feel, no one of the papers — or of the brief passages — whose genuineness has been called in question that does not bear the stamp of Poe's manner.

Accordingly, I believe we are justified in concluding that Griswold's chief delinquencies as editor consist in the minor delinquencies of careless proofreading, in a willingness to set his own judgment against Poe's in the matter of certain textual readings, and in the omission of sundry more or less important items. As editor — that is, merely as editor — he probably performed the task committed to him as well as any other American editor of his time, save possibly Lowell, could have done. It was as biographer, not as editor, that Griswold sinned against Poe.

THE BACKGROUNDS OF POE[1]

I

I⊤ is traditionally held that Poe betrays in his writings little or no touch with his times or with the land of his birth. He lived and wrote, we are told, "out of space, out of time." An English critic, writing anonymously in the *Academy* for May 14, 1910, declares that his poems, "for aught themselves have to show . . . might have been written a thousand years ago, and amid the loneliness that haunts still undiscovered poles." Both his poems and his tales, so Professor Henry A. Beers once declared, "might have been written *in vacuo* for anything American in them." [2] According to the late Mr. Hamilton Wright Mabie, "Poe stands alone in our literature, unrelated to his environment and detached from his time." [3] In the opinion of Professor Bliss Perry, he was "a timeless, placeless embodiment of technical artistry." [4] He "escapes into a phantasmal world which registers a complete divorce from his environ-

---

[1] Published in part in *Studies in Philology*, xx, 293–301 (July, 1923), under the title "Poe in Relation to his Times."

[2] *Initial Studies in American Letters*, New York, 1895, p. 173.

[3] The *Atlantic Monthly*, lxxxiv, 738 (December, 1899).

[4] *The American Spirit in Literature*, New Haven, 1918, p. 196.

[99]

ment," [1] asserts Mr. Lewis Mumford. And a similar view has repeatedly made its way into our text-books on American literature.[2]

But so extreme a view is not, I think, sustained by a thoroughgoing examination of Poe's writings. It is true that Poe transcended his environment in a good many ways. More than any other American of his day he was partial to old-world subjects and to other-world settings and situations. He made little use of American scenery, and he showed scarcely any concern in his more imaginative writings for the every-day affairs of his fellow-Americans. He cared little, moreover, so far as his writings reveal, for American occasions, and even less for our native legends and traditionary lore. And nowhere in his writings does he display any whole-hearted devotion to his country. But surely too much has been made of his detachment from time and place. He was not, I am convinced, in any true sense out of touch with his times, nor was he essentially un-American. On the contrary, he seems to me to have been pretty deeply indebted to his age; and not only does he reflect his American environment in much of what he wrote, but he also reveals in some of his writings the pecu-

[1] The *Literary Review*, April 5, 1924, p. 642. In his volume *The Golden Day* (New York, 1926, pp. 76, 77) Mr. Mumford modifies this opinion somewhat.

[2] There are, to be sure, those who have held to a contrary view. See, in particular, Woodberry, *America in Literature*, pp. 142 f.; and also, with especial reference to his Americanism, Barrett Wendell and C. Alphonso Smith, in addresses published in *The Book of the Poe Centenary*, University of Virginia, 1909, pp. 117 f., 159 f.

liar influence of Virginia and the South, where he spent most of his youth. I shall enumerate some of the ways in which he seems to me to have been indebted to his times, and I shall then give a number of particulars in which he appears to reflect an indebtedness to America and to the South.

II

In Poe's poems I am unable to find any specific reference to contemporary movements or to contemporary conditions; but an indebtedness to his times is nevertheless discoverable in virtually every poem that he wrote. For nothing is plainer than that Poe as a poet — and he is, to me, first of all a poet — belongs with the Romanticists of his time. And he belongs not alone with Coleridge, whom the ablest of his biographers has justly characterized as "the guiding genius of [his] early intellectual life," [1] but with Byron also and with Moore and with Shelley. He began his career as a poet by imitating Byron and Moore; he came a little later under the spell of Shelley; and both in his theorizing as to poetry and in the application of these theories to his own art he proclaimed himself the ardent disciple of Coleridge.

[1] Woodberry, *The Life of Poe*, Boston, 1909, I, 177. In the earlier edition of this biography (Boston, 1885, p. 93) Professor Woodberry had indeed made a more sweeping statement, — to the effect that Coleridge was the "guiding genius" of Poe's "entire intellectual life," — and Dr. F. H. Stovall, in an article on "Poe's Debt to Coleridge" (University of Texas *Studies in English*, No. 10, 1930, p. 127), maintains that the earlier judgment more nearly fits the facts.

In his "Tamerlane" and "Al Aaraaf" and "Israfel" he worked with Oriental materials; in "The Raven," "The Haunted Palace," and "Annabel Lee" he followed, even though afar off, in the footsteps of the balladists; in a dozen of his later lyrics — and notably in his rhapsodies to Mrs. Shew and Mrs. Whitman [1] — he asserted his kinship with the sentimentalists; and there is an unmistakable Gothic strain both in his earlier and in some of his later verses.[2]

In two of his poems, moreover, — *Politian* and "Eldorado," — Poe dealt with contemporary happenings, albeit this fact does not lie on the surface. The plot of *Politian*, as the poet's English biographer, Ingram, has shown,[3] was based on a sensational tragedy of ante-bellum Kentucky, the killing (in 1825) of Solomon P. Sharp by Jeroboam O. Beauchamp, followed by the hanging of Beauchamp and the suicide of his wife; while his "Eldorado" owed its immediate origin to the excitement aroused late in the forties by the discovery of gold in California. His "Al Aaraaf" I like to think of as an early protest (though but poorly made out) against the "heresy of the didactic," the poet's first bugle blast in a battle that he was to wage all his life long in behalf of the beautiful. The "Sonnet. To Science" was a protest against the notion (which had but lately been defended by Leigh Hunt in his memorable review of

[1] "To M. L. S——" and the second of his lyrics "To Helen."

[2] See, for instance, among his earlier verses, "The Sleeper," ll. 47 f., and among his later work, "The Conqueror Worm."

[3] The *Southern Magazine*, xvii, 588 ff. (November, 1875).

Keats's volume of 1820)[1] that there is no essential incompatibility between poetry and science. One of his fragments — "A Campaign Song" — is said to have been improvised for use in General Harrison's campaign for the Presidency. Three of the poems contain references to contemporary persons of note: to Napoleon in an early version of "A Dream within a Dream," to Miss Letitia E. Landon ("L. E. L.") in "An Acrostic," and to Henry T. Tuckerman in the phrase *tuckermanities* in "An Enigma." Four of his poems — "A Valentine," "An Enigma," "An Acrostic," and "Elizabeth" — reflect the contemporary fondness for puzzles and charades. And further confutation of the theory of a complete disseverance from things temporal is afforded by the poet's occasional references to relatives and friends (to his wife and Mrs. Clemm, to his mother, to Miss Herring, Mrs. Whitman, Mrs. Osgood, Mrs. Shew, Mrs. Lewis, and Mrs. Richmond) and by his constant, though often veiled, allusions to himself.

Poe's indebtedness to his times is even more palpably revealed in his stories. No one can read the American newspapers of the thirties and forties of last century without observing how often the subjects of ballooning, of voyages into remote parts of the world, of premature burial, of mesmerism, of the pestilence, and of mystification of some sort recur there. Now Poe deals with feats in aeronautics in no fewer than six of his stories: "Hans Pfaall," "The

[1] The *Indicator*, August 2 and 9, 1820.

Man that was Used Up," "The Balloon Hoax,"
"The Angel of the Odd," "The Thousand-and-
Second Tale of Scheherazade," and "Mellonta
Tauta." In four of the tales — "MS. Found in a
Bottle," "Hans Pfaall," "The Journal of Julius
Rodman," and *The Narrative of Arthur Gordon Pym*
— he deals with miraculous or mysterious voyages
into distant parts. Six of the tales — "Berenice,"
"Loss of Breath," "Ligeia," "The Fall of the
House of Usher," "The Premature Burial," and
"Some Words with a Mummy" — have to do with
burial before death or with restoring the dead to life.
Two — "Mesmeric Revelation" and "The Strange
Case of M. Valdemar" — are concerned with mesmerism, and still others touch incidentally upon
mesmerism. Four of the stories — "King Pest,"
"Shadow," "The Mask of the Red Death," and
"The Sphinx" — have to do with the pestilence
(cholera) which raged in the United States in the
eighteen-thirties. Others — as "Hans Pfaall" and
"The Balloon Hoax" — illustrate the contemporary
craze for mystification and hoaxing. And still others
take account of some contemporary fashion in dress
or of some reform movement of the time. Thus
mention is made in one story of the fashion of
wearing hoop-skirts,[1] and in three tales — "The
Thousand-and-Second Tale of Scheherazade," "The
Spectacles," and "Mellonta Tauta" — of the enor-
mous bustles in vogue in Poe's day as articles of

[1] *Poe's Works*, VI, 60.

feminine adornment. In one of the earliest of the tales, "How to Write a Blackwood Article," Poe pokes fun at reform movements; in "Never Bet the Devil Your Head" he represents his hero as having taken the "temperance pledge"; and in "The System of Dr. Tarr and Prof. Fether," a farce depicting conditions in an asylum for the insane, he appears to echo the contemporary interest in humanitarian activities in that direction.

Some fifteen of the tales refer more or less specifically to Poe's own century. The extraordinary feat of "Mr. Monck Mason" and "Mr. Harrison Ainsworth" in crossing the Atlantic in a balloon — of which we have a minutely detailed account in "The Balloon Hoax" — is represented as having been accomplished on April 6, 7, and 8, 1844, a few days before the publication of the account in the New York *Sun*. The events recorded in "A Tale of the Ragged Mountains" and in "Some Words with a Mummy" are associated with the year 1845. "The Sphinx" purports to record an incident that took place in New York in 1832. Arthur Gordon Pym in the story of that name is represented as setting out from New Bedford for his fateful journey into the South Seas in June, 1827. Other tales are assigned to the nineteenth century without explicit mention of the year; and still others are associated with the closing years of the eighteenth century.[1]

[1] Among incidental references to matters of contemporary interest are the mention of the pedestrian feat of Captain Barclay Allardice in

TALES

Fully a dozen of the tales contain references to contemporary notabilities, English and American, — among those mentioned being Coleridge, Carlyle, William Godwin, Horace Smith, Lady Morgan, the Prince of Wales, Thomas Jefferson, John Randolph of Roanoke, Commodore Maury, John Jacob Astor, Washington Irving, and the poets Longfellow and Emerson; and still other tales contain references to periodicals of Poe's time, — including *Blackwood's*, *Fraser's*, *Bentley's*, the *Edinburgh Review*, the *North American Review*, the *Knickerbocker*, the *Home Journal*, the *Brother Jonathan*, and the *Saturday Evening Post*. In five of the tales [1] Poe touches upon the form of government lately set up in America, referring facetiously (as I believe), in two of them, to difficulties and abuses that had already been encountered in guiding the ship of state.[2] In one of the later stories, "The Elk," he speaks disapprovingly of the rising tide of industrialism in America, though in another late story, "The Thousand-and-Second Tale of Scheherazade," he writes with enthusiasm of the recent accomplishments in the natural sciences and in mechanical engineering. In five of the stories

1809 (in the tale "Loss of Breath") and the allusion to the law-suit against the Philadelphian Captain Daniel Mann, much in the newspapers during the year 1839, in "The Man that was Used Up." For these and other items I am indebted to an article by Miss Cornelia Varner in the *Journal of English and Germanic Philology*, XXXI, 77–80 (January, 1933).

[1] "The Colloquy of Monos and Una," "Mellonta Tauta," "The Sphinx," "The Business Man," and "Some Words with a Mummy."

[2] *Poe's Works*, IV, 203; VI, 208–209.

he takes a fling of some sort at Transcendentalism,[1] being most severe in "Never Bet the Devil Your Head," where he sneeringly remarks of Mr. Toby Dammit, "It is not impossible that he was affected with the transcendentals," and adds sarcastically: "I am not well enough versed, however, in the diagnosis of this disease to speak with decision on the point." [2] In several other stories he adverts to the German mystics of his day and their philosophy. In "X-ing a Paragrab" he apparently endeavors to settle an old score with the city of Boston, which had dealt with him ungraciously, as he thought, on the occasion of his visit to that city in the fall of 1845. In other stories he makes reference to contemporary fads, as phrenology,[3] and cryptography, and landscape gardening; several times he adverts to the custom of blood-letting, once to the use of the leech for a like purpose.

Perhaps as many as half of Poe's tales were based, in whole or in part, on contemporary happenings or were suggested by contemporary publications of some sort.[4] "The Mystery of Marie Rogêt," for instance, is confessedly an elaboration of a sensational murder mystery of the early forties. "Von Kempelen and his Discovery," like the poem "Eldorado," grew

[1] "How to Write a Blackwood Article," "Loss of Breath," "Some Words with a Mummy," "Never Bet the Devil Your Head," and "The Literary Life of Thingum Bob, Esq."

[2] *Poe's Works*, iv, 220.

[3] Cf. Edward Hungerford, "Poe and Phrenology," *American Literature*, ii, 209 f. (November, 1930).

[4] See below, pp. 164 f.

out of the gold excitement of '49, being in this instance, so Poe told Duyckinck,[1] a quiz on the subject. "Diddling Considered as One of the Exact Sciences" evidently took its cue, at least so far as the title is concerned, from James Kenney's farce, "Raising the Wind" (1803), Kenney's title being used by Poe as a sub-title for the story upon its first publication.[2] Similarly the title of his farce "Why the Little Frenchman Wears his Hand in a Sling" was perhaps suggested by George P. Morris's story "The Little Frenchman and his Water Lots" (1839). "Mystification" is in some fashion a satire on the contemporary custom of duelling; and four other tales — "How to Write a Blackwood Article," "A Predicament," "X-ing a Paragrab," and "The Literary Life of Thingum Bob, Esq." — are directed against the whimsies of contemporary editors.[3] "Three Sundays in a Week," as has recently been shown, is but a reworking of an anecdote from the Philadelphia *Ledger*.[4] Bulwer was drawn on for at

[1] *Poe's Works*, XVII, 341.

[2] The Philadelphia *Saturday Courier*, October 14, 1843.

[3] "Lionizing" is said to have been intended as a quiz on N. P. Willis: see *Poe's Works*, VIII, x. "Loss of Breath" was evidently meant as a burlesque on current types of magazine fiction (see in this connection F. L. Pattee, *The Development of the American Short Story*, New York, 1923, pp. 122 f., and James Southall Wilson in the *American Mercury*, XXIV, 215 f. [October, 1931]). And most of the rest of Poe's early stories cater to the contemporary taste for the terrible, the fantastical, and the metaphysical (see Napier Wilt, "Poe's Attitude toward his Tales," *Modern Philology*, XXV, 101 f. [August, 1927], and Miss Margaret Alterton's thesis, *Origins of Poe's Critical Theory*, Iowa City, 1925, *passim*).

[4] See Miss F. N. Cherry in *American Literature*, II, 232 f. (November, 1930).

least two of the stories, and Irving clearly enough
for two others. Disraeli, Harrison Ainsworth,
Horace Smith, Macaulay, Balzac, and E. T. A.
Hoffmann likewise appear to have furnished grist
for his mill.

That Poe's tales, moreover, despite a strain of
realism here and there, were, like the poems, a
product of the Romantic Movement, is so obvious
as scarcely to call for demonstration. Suffice it to
say that Poe makes use, in one or another of his tales,
of very nearly all the conventional devices that distinguish the work of the Gothic romancer, — the
machinery of trap-doors and subterranean chambers,
of secret passages and decayed castles, of ghostly
apparitions, of trances, of cataleptic attacks, of life
after death, — and that he exhibits virtually all the
abstract qualities that we associate with Romanticism, including the elements of mystery and terror,
the morbid, the grotesque, the strange, the remote,
and the extravagant.

But if there were no other evidence of Poe's touch
with his times, we should still have most conclusive
evidence of his closeness to his age in his critical and
miscellaneous writings. These are mainly book-
reviews, and hence are by their very nature as genuinely contemporary as are the pages of one of our
literary weeklies of the present time.

In his book-reviews Poe passed judgment on very
nearly every writer of importance belonging to his
generation, — on Dickens and Bulwer and Disraeli,

on Macaulay and Leigh Hunt and Southey, on Coleridge, on Mrs. Browning, on Tennyson, to mention but a few among his English contemporaries; on Irving and Bryant and Hawthorne and Lowell and Longfellow and Willis and Cooper and Kennedy and Simms and Margaret Fuller and Mrs. Osgood, to mention a few Americans. Here we have a painstaking review of Bulwer's *Night and Morning* or a bitterly satirical notice of Theodore S. Fay's *Norman Leslie*, there the famous essay on Hawthorne's *Twice-Told Tales*; here a paper in which his fellow-critics are reprimanded for their dimness of vision in not recognizing the superior gifts of Tennyson, there the famous advance notice of *Barnaby Rudge*, in which he astonished Dickens by outlining the course which the plot of his novel was to take; here the very minute dissection of one of Mrs. Browning's volumes, which led Mrs. Browning to remark that he had "so obviously and thoroughly read [her] poems as to be a wonder among critics"; [1] there the contemptuous notice of Dawes's *Damascus* or the slashing criticism of the long since forgotten poems of Ellery Channing.

Here, too, it was that Poe aired his views and vented his spleen on what he conceived to be the chief besetting literary evils of the day, — on literary puffery and log-rolling, on "slipshodiness" [2] in

---

[1] See her letter of May 12, 1845, to R. H. Horne, reprinted by Harrison, *Poe's Works*, xvii, 387.

[2] Poe's spelling: *Poe's Works*, xvi, 80.

style, on imitation and plagiarism, on didacticism, on a blind subservience to foreign critical opinion, and on an inordinate esteem of one's own things.

And here also — for his reviews dealt with all manner of men and things — he touches on a number of subjects that are not primarily literary in character. In three of his early papers he writes, with evident sincerity, in defense of Negro slavery,[1] in one of them dwelling on the happy relations that existed between the slave and his master,[2] in another recording the opinion that most of the pictures that had been made of slavery were drawn "in red ochre."[3] In one of the latest of his reviews he makes a savage attack on Lowell for what he characterizes as his "fanaticism about slavery." [4] In another he speaks of "the cabal of the *North American Review*"; [5] and he remarks in that connection that "it is high time that the literary South took its own interests into its own charge." In other papers he complains that the contemporary system of anonymous reviewing is a "most despicable and cowardly practice," [6] and declares that the stage criticism of the day was in "the control of illiterate mountebanks." [7] In one of his "Marginalia" written shortly before his death, he remarks with reference to the growth of magazine

[1] See the uncollected review of Joseph H. Ingraham's *The South-West* in the *Southern Literary Messenger*, II, 122–123 (January, 1836), and see also *ibid.*, pp. 337–339 (April), 511 f. (July).

[2] *Ibid.*, p. 338. [3] *Ibid.*, p. 122.

[4] *Ibid.*, xv, 190 (March, 1849).

[5] *Poe's Works*, xvi, 142.

[6] *Ibid.*, p. 153. [7] *Ibid.*, viii, 322

literature in his day that "it is but a sign of the times, an indication of an era in which men are forced upon the curt, the condensed, the well-digested in place of the voluminous"; [1] and in another late paper he declares that "the whole tendency of the age is Magazine-ward." [2] In an article written in 1841 he speaks of "the present absurd rage for lecturing," [3] and in a paper written a little later he characterizes the public address then in vogue as a compound of "stale wisdom, overdone sentiment, schoolboy classicalities, bad English, worse Latin, and wholesale rhodomontade." [4]

In a somewhat less tangible way he exhibits his nearness to his times by his fondness for "cutting and slashing," — a weakness that he may well have caught from Gifford and Jeffrey, but that had already established itself pretty securely in the political life of America. And the same may be said of his obsession about imitation and plagiarism, matters that were constantly to the fore in the periodicals of his day, as well in England as in America.

In Poe's miscellaneous writings, moreover, — his news articles, his editorials, his "Marginalia," his "Autography" and similar papers, and his *Eureka*, — we have a further body of matter that is almost exclusively contemporary in nature. He treats here of such subjects as the pay of authors in his day, the best methods of street-paving, imprisonment for

[1] *Poe's Works*, xvi, 82.   [2] *Ibid.*, p. 117.
[3] *Ibid.*, x, 145.   [4] *Ibid.*, p. 57.

debt, the law of copyright, early nineteenth-century movements in behalf of prohibition and temperance, the attitude of the time to the skeptic, Babbage's calculating machine, "the uproar about Pusey," schemes for crossing the Atlantic in an air-ship, Leverrier's discovery of Neptune, the growth in America of an "aristocracy of dollars," the lack of taste and the rage for "glitter" in American household decoration; or he caters to the contemporary interest in ciphers and cryptographs, offering in one of his papers to unravel any cipher that may be proposed to him; or he collects the autographs of distinguished living Americans, and dilates audaciously upon them; or he records the weekly gossip about plays and players in New York City; or he makes bold, in his *Eureka*, to wrestle with such questions as the origin of the universe and the evolution of matter, questions that were agitating the minds of more than one of the greatest of his contemporaries.[1]

III

Poe's indebtedness to his section [2] — to pass now to the second of the twin problems under consideration — is less obvious than his debt to his times, and is

[1] See F. D. Bond, "Poe as an Evolutionist," the *Popular Science Monthly*, LXXI, 267 ff. (September, 1907).

[2] I ought to say at once that in speaking of Poe's section I am thinking not alone of the South, to which indeed he professed to belong (see his statement in a letter to F. W. Thomas of June 26, 1841 [*Poe's Works*, XVII, 91], "I am a Virginian, at least I call myself one"), and where he spent his most impressionable years, but of America at large, or, more precisely, of the Atlantic seaboard. Though Southern by temperament

also, I think, less significant. But there is, for all that, a good deal, especially in his prose, that cannot readily be explained except by the circumstance that he lived his life in America.

In his poems, it must be granted, such references as he makes to his local environment are few and indefinite. Possibly he refers — but if so, very vaguely — to the city of Richmond in his "Sonnet. To Zante." It may be that he refers to Baltimore, as has been suggested, in the opening lines of "Annabel Lee." [1] There is a veiled reference to a flower-garden at Mrs. Whitman's home in his later lyric "To Helen." But the only specific reference to his own land that I can find in his poems is the altogether conventional allusion to America in the seventh scene of his play *Politian*, in which he speaks of America as

a land new found —
Miraculously found by one of Genoa —
A thousand leagues within the golden west.[2]

Be it said, however, in explanation of the fewness of such references that it was one of Poe's favorite critical doctrines that the lyric — and all save two or three of his poems are lyrics — should not con-

as well as by early training, he spent his most active years in the Middle States, — six years in Philadelphia and at least seven years in New York City, — and some of his writings were conditioned upon this fact. *The Literati*, for instance, would scarcely have been written if he had not been living in New York, nor "The Elk" if he had not lived at some time in Philadelphia.

[1] The *South Atlantic Quarterly*, xi, 175 f. (April, 1912).

[2] *Politian*, edited by T. O. Mabbott, Richmond, 1923, p. 26.

cern itself with the local and the definite, but should be characterized by indefiniteness, — or, as he liked to phrase it, by "indefinitiveness." [1] Consistently with this belief he laid the scene of most of his poems either in a spirit-world of some sort (as in "Al Aaraaf," "Eldorado," and "Dreamland") or in some symbolic and dimly veiled situation (as in "Stanzas," "Eulalie," and "Bridal Ballad"); and the characters that he introduces into his poems are, with unimportant exceptions, of the same shadowy nature.[2]

Accordingly, such indebtedness to his section as is to be found in Poe's verses must be sought, not in the introduction of local scenery or incident, but — and this applies only to the South — in his very scrupulous avoidance of the didactic in his poems (in which he associates himself with Cavalier Virginia as against the semi-Puritan New England of his day), and also — if we may adopt a suggestion once made by the poet Stedman [3] — in his emphasis upon simple musical effects, in which Stedman would trace the influence of the Negro.[4]

While, however, Poe's indebtedness to his local

[1] See, for instance, *Poe's Works*, VII, xliii; x, 41 f.; XVI, 28 f., 137 f.

[2] The poet's mere references to certain friends and relatives (as Mrs. Osgood, Mrs. Lewis, and Mrs. Clemm) constitute almost the sole exceptions.

[3] *Poets of America*, p. 251. See also in this connection Hervey Allen, *Israfel*, p. 60.

[4] Professor C. Alphonso Smith finds, also, an echo of his Americanism in his discipleship of Coleridge, which he maintains was characteristic of Virginia and the South (see *The Book of the Poe Centenary*, p. 174).

environment is but dimly discoverable in his poems, it is abundantly evident in his stories, and in his critical and miscellaneous essays. "The Gold-Bug," for instance, the best-known of his stories, has its setting in the neighborhood of Charleston, South Carolina, while its action centres about the traditionary American hero Captain Kidd.[1] It was, indeed, one of the conditions of admission to the contest in which this story was awarded first prize that the scene should be laid in America and the action should be concerned with some peculiarly American situation or incident. Besides "The Gold-Bug" there are four other stories whose setting is in the South, — namely, "The Oblong Box," in which Charleston serves as the point of departure for the undertaking with which the story has to do; "The Balloon Hoax," in which Charleston is the point at which the main action culminates; "A Tale of the Ragged Mountains," the events of which occur in or near Charlottesville, Virginia, where Poe had once attended college; and "The Premature Burial," which records an incident said to have taken place near Richmond. "The Journal of Julius Rodman," moreover, in which Poe associates himself with the goodly company of those who have dealt with pioneering in the West, gives an account of an expedition which had its beginning in an obscure town in Kentucky.[2]

[1] An American only by adoption, I grant, but in fiction and literary tradition associated only with America, I believe.

[2] In a review published in the *Southern Literary Messenger* as far back as 1836, Poe remarks prophetically: "Who can say, viewing the rapid

And at least seven of the stories are more or less definitely associated with some section of the North. "The Elk" describes a scene on the Wissahickon in the vicinity of Philadelphia; "The Sphinx," "Mellonta Tauta," "X-ing a Paragrab," and "The Strange Case of M. Valdemar" are all associated with the city of New York; "Landor's Cottage" has to do with a rural scene not far from the same city; and the initial incident of *Arthur Gordon Pym* takes place off the coast of Massachusetts near the city of New Bedford. The plot underlying "The Mystery of Marie Rogêt," moreover, though its scene is laid in Paris, has to do in reality, as Poe tells us in his foot-notes, with a murder committed at Weehawken, New Jersey.[1]

There are, besides, incidental references in a dozen of Poe's stories to American places, — to Canada, to Niagara Falls, to the Hudson River, to Saratoga, Albany, and Utica, to New Bedford and Nantucket, to Boston and Concord, to Providence, to the Schuylkill River, to Baltimore, to Harper's Ferry, to Charlottesville and Abingdon, to New Orleans and

growth of our population, that the Rocky Mountains shall forever constitute the western boundary of our republic, or that it shall not stretch its dominion from sea to sea" (*Poe's Works*, IX, 88).

[1] The heroine of "Landor's Cottage," it may be added, is none other than the poet's friend, Mrs. Annie Richmond, of Lowell, Massachusetts, to whom he addressed his lyric "For Annie." "The Oval Portrait" is said to have been suggested by a portrait made by Robert M. Sully, a Richmond artist (see Miss Mary E. Phillips, *Poe — the Man*, p. 691). And "Eleonora," like "Annabel Lee," has been held to have reference to the scene of Poe's early love-making in Baltimore (see Ingram, p. 110, and W. F. Melton in the *South Atlantic Quarterly*, XI, 175 f.).

the Mississippi, to the Ohio and the Delaware, to Ocracoke Inlet and Cape Hatteras and Roanoke Island, to Yorktown and Bunker Hill, to a Louisiana landscape, to the Black Hills of Dakota, to the Capitol at Washington, to Thomas Jefferson's home "Monticello," to the Bowling Green Fountain in New York City and to the Mammoth Cave of Kentucky, to a petrified forest in Texas. In addition to the contemporary American notabilities already mentioned in my effort to demonstrate Poe's indebtedness to his time, a score of lesser Americans are referred to, including General Zachary Taylor, Thomas H. Benton, George Denison Prentice, Lewis Gaylord Clark, Rufus W. Griswold, Henry T. Tuckerman, Orestes A. Brownson, John Neal, and S. F. B. Morse. Negroes figure in the background of eight of the stories, — namely, "The Gold-Bug," "The Oblong Box," "The Elk," "How to Write a Blackwood Article" and "A Predicament," "The Spectacles," *Arthur Gordon Pym*, and "The Journal of Julius Rodman";[1] and half a dozen or more Indian tribes are mentioned in one or another of the stories, including the Upsarokas, the Kickapoos, the Sioux, the Omahas, and the Choctaws.

An echo of the old-time animosity of the South towards New England is to be caught in the reference, in one of the late stories, to "the odious old woods of Concord"[2] — evidently a back-handed

[1] In several of these stories, Poe tries his hand at the Negro dialect, though without much success.

[2] *Poe's Works*, vi, 233.

slap at Emerson — and in the mention of making "nutmegs out of pine-knots,"[1] as also in his thrusts at Transcendentalism. Boston is several times referred to contemptuously as "Frogpondium," and once, in a late revision of an early story, as a city with "its upper end lost . . . *parmi les nues.*"[2] On the other hand, Poe rises above any sectional feeling that he may have harbored when he employs a stanza from "A Psalm of Life" as the headpiece of "The Tell-Tale Heart," and he refers to the singing of "Yankee Doodle" in "Dr. Tarr and Prof. Fether." In one of the stories he makes mention of the "Bowie knife," in another of "fire-eaters," and in yet another he uses the Jacksonian phrase "blood and thunder."

Poe reflects his Americanism, also, both in the foresightedness that he displays in his imaginary accounts of aeronautic feats in "The Balloon Hoax" and in "Mellonta Tauta," and likewise in his prophecies, in "Mellonta Tauta," as to the material developments that were to come about in the course of the next century in New York City. Professor C. Alphonso Smith maintains that Poe shows himself peculiarly American in the inventive skill that he exhibited in the construction of his stories.[3] So, also, Mr. Lewis Mumford finds in him "the literary equivalent of the industrialist and the pioneer," and declares that in his emphasis on terror and cruelty he

[1] *Ibid.,* IV, 123.   [2] *Ibid.,* II, 199.
[3] *The Book of the Poe Centenary,* pp. 163 f.

betrays the influence of pioneer life and the atmosphere that surrounded it.[1]

And is it too much to say, with Mr. Paul Elmer More, that Poe in his concern for moral questions, however superficial it may have been, — in his dwelling on the workings of the conscience, for instance, and on the innate perversity of human nature, and even in his unearthly visions (to adopt Mr. More's own words), — reflects in some measure his American origin?[2]

And in Poe's critical and miscellaneous essays — to bring my cataloguing speedily to an end — there is not only abundant evidence of his interest in the intellectual and literary life of America in his day, but also convincing proof of his interest in political and industrial conditions, in America's commerce, in America's discoveries on sea and land, and in

[1] *The Golden Day*, pp. 76, 77. — The late Professor Woodberry suggests, in his *America in Literature*, p. 147, that Poe's highly idealized heroines, such as "Ligeia" and "Madeline Usher" and "Morella," owed something perhaps to types with which the poet was acquainted in the South; and this may be, for the South of Poe's time exhibited (I dare say) more of sentiment and more of glamor than characterized the more serious and practical-minded folk of the North; but I incline to believe that no such character as Poe depicted in these heroines, however attractive they may be, ever existed outside of the imagination — or of the pages of a book. His debt, if any, was, I suspect, rather to Bulwer or to Scott or to the idealized fiction that he found in the periodicals of his day.

[2] *Shelburne Essays*, 1st Series, p. 53. Mr. More, in contrasting Poe and Hawthorne with the Gothic Romanticists of England and Germany, dwells on the "genuineness" of the Romanticism of Poe and Hawthorne, and remarks that "their work is the last efflorescence of a tradition handed down . . . from the earliest colonial days," and that their "unearthly visions . . . are deep-rooted in American history." They wrote, observes Mr. More (p. 70), "from the depths of this profound moral experience of their people."

multifarious other matters relating to America's social and material well-being. Fully a third of his reviews and critical notices have to do with books by American writers, in which he allots praise and blame impartially to Northerner and Southerner alike, save in so far as he is severe in some of his reviews upon certain New Englanders, being moved, it may be, by sectional prejudice or by something of jealousy. It is in these papers, and especially in his reviews in the *Southern Literary Messenger*, that he exhibits most plainly his Southern bias. In an uncollected book-notice he remarks that there once existed in Virginia a society "as absolutely aristocratical as any in Europe." [1] In several of his early papers he adverts either directly or indirectly to the Southerner's traditional chivalry and sense of honor. In another early review he remarks, with less adroitness than was usual with him, that "*we* [in the South] do not put the names of our fine women in the newspapers." [2] In another early paper he defends Virginia against the charge of disloyalty to England in the days of the Commonwealth.[3] He commends Virginia for having established its University under State auspices.[4] He writes with evident pride of the history and traditions of William and Mary, and remarks that to this ancient college is especially due "the high political character of Virginia." [5] At the

[1] *Burton's Gentleman's Magazine*, v, 228 (October, 1839).
[2] The *Southern Literary Messenger*, i, 520 f. (May, 1835).
[3] *Poe's Works*, viii, 243.
[4] *Ibid.*, p. 323.   [5] *Ibid.*, ix, 193.

same time he reproaches Virginia for her failure to establish a system of public schools, pointing out that the South lagged far behind New England in this particular;[1] or he complains that Virginia "has manifested too little of that public spirit which has animated other communities."[2] In one of his papers he deplores the literary supineness of the South and the Southern tactlessness "in all matters relating to the making of money."[3] In another early review he admits that a "vast deal of jealousy and misapprehension" exists between the North and the South.[4] And in an early editorial he gives the history of what he calls "Lynch's Law," and remarks that this so-called law has had "terrible and deeply to be lamented consequences."[5]

Against America as a nation he brings the accusation that it had allowed a "perpetual and unhealthy excitement about the forms and machinery of governmental action" so to absorb its attention "as to exclude in a strange degree all care of the proper *results* of good government — the happiness of a people."[6] He speaks of "our innumerable moral, physical, and social absurdities" as a people;[7] and of our intolerance and our sensitiveness to criticism

[1] The *Southern Literary Messenger*, II, 67 (December, 1835).
[2] *Poe's Works*, VIII, 212.   [3] *Ibid.*, XIII, 95.
[4] The *Southern Literary Messenger*, II, 122 (January, 1836).
[5] *Ibid.*, p. 389. This essay does not appear in any collected edition of Poe's writings, but it is assigned to Poe by B. B. Minor (*The Southern Literary Messenger* [New York, 1905], p. 45), and circumstantial evidence tells strongly in favor of its authenticity.
[6] *Poe's Works*, IX, 54.   [7] *Ibid.*, p. 1.

by foreigners. In a review of one of Cooper's books
he declares that "we are a bull-headed and prejudiced people, and it were well if we had a few more
of the stamp of Mr. Cooper who would feel themselves at liberty to tell us so to our teeth." [1] In another review he declares that "as a literary people
we are one vast perambulating humbug." [2] But he
praises Americans for their "cool self-possession,
courage, and enduring fortitude," and for their possession of a "mental elasticity which liberal institu-
tions inspire"; [3] or he notes that they have "a taste
for science and a spirit of research," [4] and he pleads
for an "enlightened liberality" which shall provide
maritime commercial activities, declaring at the same
time that America has a treasury which can afford
to "remunerate scientific research," and that it is
America's duty, holding as it does "a high rank in
the scale of nations, to contribute a large share to
that aggregate of useful knowledge, which is the
common property of all." [5]

Among still other subjects of local import that he
adverts to in his essays are the American love of
gain, the degrading spirit of utilitarianism abroad in
the land, "which sees in mountains and waterfalls
only quarries and manufacturing sites"; "our national degradation and subserviency to British opin-

[1] *Ibid.*, p. 163.
[2] *Ibid.*, x, 185 f.
[3] The *Southern Literary Messenger*, ii, 587 f. (August, 1836).
[4] *Poe's Works*, ix, 50.
[5] The *Southern Literary Messenger*, ii, 588 (August, 1836).

ion"; "the dearth of satire in America"; the "universal corruption and rigmarole" in our literary criticism. Or he touches on such miscellaneous subjects as the "gong at Astor's," "Barnum's baboons," the inferiority of "Yankee razors," the attractiveness of the White Sulphur Springs, the "briar-encumbered graveyard at Jamestown," the iniquities chargeable against Jefferson on the score of his religious opinions. In a series of letters written in 1844 for an obscure Pennsylvania paper, the *Columbia Spy*,[1] he presents a body of gossip and small talk about the "doings" day by day in New York City, — in the police courts, along the docks, in the business sections, — mentioning among other things a "raree show" at the house of "Messrs. Tiffany, Young, and Ellis," at which were to be seen all sorts of "knicknackatory"; and taking occasion incidentally to record his disapproval of the recently constructed Bowling Green Fountain and his abhorrence of the street-cries of Brooklyn and of the average Brooklyn dwelling-house, which reminds him of "silvered gingerbread." And in his latter years, when hard put to it to keep the wolf away from the door, he condescended, in an evil hour, to publish to the world his "honest opinions" of some thirty-eight of his fellow New Yorkers aspiring to literary fame,[2]

---

[1] See *Doings of Gotham*, ed. J. E. Spannuth and T. O. Mabbott, Pottsville, Pennsylvania, 1929.

[2] See his series of papers entitled *The Literati* published in *Godey's Lady's Book* in 1846 (*Poe's Works*, xv, 1–137). See also his "Autography" (*ibid.*, pp. 139 f.), in which he comments in somewhat similar fashion,

and thus stirred up a hornet's nest that was not to subside until long after Poe had been laid in his grave.

IV

Such is the evidence as I find it. In the light of the evidence it seems to me sheer folly to try to maintain that Poe was but little interested in his environment and that he owed little to it. It is true that his debt to his environment, whether in time or place, is less obvious in his more imaginative work than is the case with most of his American contemporaries — and to this circumstance, I suspect, is to be traced very largely the popular misconception which I am now combating; but even in his most imaginative work, in his best poems and tales, there is much that relates him to his times, and there is not a little in most of them that also relates him to the land in which he lived and wrought. And if we may take into account his less imaginative work, his critical and miscellaneous prose writings, it becomes at once convincingly evident that Poe was as truly related to his times and as clearly in touch with things American as were more than one of his contemporaries whose preoccupation with the things of the time and of the nation would never be called in question.

but less audaciously, upon upwards of a hundred other Americans of his day.

SELF–REVELATION IN POE'S
POEMS AND TALES

I

THE chief sources of first-hand information about Poe's life and personality are his letters.[1] These are regrettably few, scarcely more than two hundred in all, and a good many of them are perfunctory in nature. Only one letter to his wife survives; and only four letters, I believe, to his mother-in-law, his "more than mother," Mrs. Clemm, have come down to us. But there are letters that conveniently furnish us with the genealogy of the poet, that give information about his relations with his immediate family and about his home life;[2] letters that reveal his poverty, his pride, his impulsiveness and rebelliousness, his moodiness and vacillation, his misanthropy; that tell of his bickerings and squabbles, of his occasional philanderings, of his indulging — alas! too often — in intoxicants, of an attack of insanity (as he alleges),

[1] The bulk of these appear in the seventeenth volume of *Poe's Works* as edited by Professor James A. Harrison (New York, 1902), but a good many others are to be found in the life of Poe by Professor George E. Woodberry (Boston, 1909).

[2] There is nothing that reveals to us more surely the human side of the poet's nature than his letter of April 7, 1844, to Mrs. Clemm (*Poe's Works*, XVII, 165 f.), nothing that shows more convincingly his essential manliness of character than his letter of December 30, 1846, to N. P. Willis (*ibid.*, pp. 274 f.).

of an attempt at suicide, of the physical deterioration that marked his closing years. We have a volume of letters called out by his ill-starred friendship with Mrs. Sarah Helen Whitman,[1] letters so intimate and so impassioned as to beget doubts as to the wisdom of their having been confided to the public; and another and more important volume, the so-called "Valentine Letters," [2] covering the most eventful years of his life, that were unwisely, one must think, withheld from the public until very lately, letters that tell of his early life in Richmond and Baltimore, about his career at Charlottesville and at West Point, about his momentous quarrel with his foster-father in 1827, about his life in the army, about the mysterious years that followed his expulsion from West Point.

Much may be learned, also, from his book-reviews

---

[1] *The Last Letters of Edgar Allan Poe to Sarah Helen Whitman*, ed. James A. Harrison, New York, 1909.

[2] *Edgar Allan Poe Letters . . . in the Valentine Museum, Richmond, Virginia*, ed. Mary Newton Stanard, Philadelphia, 1925. Among the most important of these letters are two written to John Allan after their quarrel in March, 1827 (pp. 55 f., 63 f.), and the long letter (pp. 253 f.) written to John Allan in January, 1831, in which the poet reproaches his foster-father for his niggardly provision for him during his stay at the University of Virginia and makes pathetic confession of his irregularities while there and subsequently. Of immense importance, too, for the story of his early life are the letters, letter-books, and other documents from the office of Ellis and Allan (now preserved in the Library of Congress, but not given to the public until more than fifty years after the poet's death), a welter of old papers in which appear numerous references to Poe and which reflect very fully the atmosphere in which he grew up. See for these *Modern Language Notes*, xxv, 127–128 (April, 1910), the *Sewanee Review*, xx, 201–212 (April, 1912), and the *Dial*, lx, 143–146 (February 17, 1916).

and his critical essays, — first of all, with respect to his creed as critic and as to his reading, but much also as to his intellectual powers and attainments, his interest in science and exploration, and as to his concern about the industrial and economic problems of his age. In an early review — to mention a few of the more personal of his critical papers — he recalls his delight as a boy in poring over the pages of *Robinson Crusoe*,[1] in another he confides to us that the reading of certain of the Elizabethan and Caroline lyrists made his "blood tingle," [2] in another he tells of his acquaintance with Chief Justice Marshall and of his admiration for him,[3] and in still others of his attitude to the Negro and to slavery. Here also are displayed his prejudices as a critic, his hobbies and his crotchets, — as his mania for exposing literary theft, his impatience with literary puffery and with subservience to foreign tastes and fashions, his abhorrence of didactics.

A good deal may be gleaned, too, from his miscellaneous prose essays, — from *Eureka* as to his interest in metaphysics and philosophy and as to certain transcendental leanings, from sundry papers in *Graham's* and other Philadelphia periodicals as to his interest in puzzles and in secret writing, from various hack articles in *Burton's Gentleman's Magazine* as to his interest in mechanical invention and in sports and pastimes, from a series of articles in the *Columbia Spy* as to his acquaintance with the gossip

---

[1] *Poe's Works*, VIII, 169.   [2] *Ibid.*, IX, 96 f.   [3] *Ibid.*, VIII, 114 f.

of the streets of New York City and as to his readiness to capitalize such odds and ends for journalistic purposes. In other papers he admits us into his workshop, and imparts to us the secrets of his craft.

His letters and his essays are, then, autobiographical throughout. Whether there is much of autobiography in his more imaginative work, in his poems and tales, is by no means so clear and has long been a matter of debate among the poet's critics and biographers. Some have held that he reflects but little of himself in his poems and his tales. This is the view, for example, of Camille Mauclair, who insists that Poe was extraordinarily objective in his writings, and that this is among his distinguishing traits as an artist.[1] So, too, Professor Napier Wilt warns us against reading into "every detail of [Poe's] writing some conscious or unconscious expression of his inner life."[2] And Professor William Minto, as far back as 1880, declared that too much had already been made of the personal note in Poe's writings.[3] On the other hand, there have been those who have held that the poems and tales of Poe are exceptionally self-revealing. Such, in effect, was the view of Poe's English biographer, John H. Ingram;[4] such was the view of the poet and critic E. C. Stedman, who held with respect to Poe's tales that the "central

[1] See Camille Mauclair, *Le Génie d'Edgar Poe*, Paris [1925], pp. 25 f.
[2] Napier Wilt, "Poe's Attitude toward his Tales: A New Document," *Modern Philology*, XXV, 101 (August, 1927).
[3] The *Fortnightly Review*, XXXIV, 74 (July 1, 1880).
[4] *The Life and Letters of Edgar Allan Poe*, London, 1880, p. 121.

[129]

figure" there, "however disguised, is always the image of the romancer himself"; [1] much the same view has been advanced by the lamented Mr. W. C. Brownell; [2] while the French critic M. Remy de Gourmont gives it as his opinion that Poe is the most subjective of all our poets: "le plus subjectif des poètes subjectifs." [3] The truth doubtless lies somewhere between these two extremes — but not midway, I am bound to believe. So sweeping a generalization as M. de Gourmont makes could surely not be sustained. Is Poe more subjective, for instance, than the author of *Leaves of Grass*, or than Lord Byron? But the truth, I am persuaded, lies more nearly with those who find in the poems and tales a large element of self-revelation than with those who find there but little of self-unfolding. In view of the clash of opinion on the subject, I have been moved to undertake a fresh examination of the matter and to go into it somewhat more in detail than has heretofore been attempted. I set down below the evidence as I find it. In the main, I have restricted myself to matters that are either obvious or (as I see them) readily demonstrable, but I have not been able to resist the temptation to indulge here and there in something of speculation.

[1] E. C. Stedman, *Poets of America*, Boston, 1885, p. 261.

[2] W. C. Brownell, *American Prose Masters*, New York, 1909, p. 234.

[3] Remy de Gourmont, *Promenades Littéraires*, Première Série, Paris, 1904, p. 361.

II

In Poe's poems I can find but few specific references
to the objective facts of the poet's life. There is, first
of all, the explicit mention of his own mother, of his
devotion to her, and of her early death, in his sonnet "To My Mother." In the same poem we have
also an avowal of his devotion to his wife and to his
wife's mother, Mrs. Clemm. Other poems are addressed to one or another of his friends: "To F——,"
"To F——s S. O——d," and "A Valentine," to
Mrs. Frances Sargent Osgood; [1] the later "To Helen,"
to Mrs. Sarah Helen Whitman; "To M. L. S——"
and "To —— —— ——," to Mrs. Marie Louise
Shew; "An Enigma," to Mrs. S. Anna Lewis; and
"For Annie," to Mrs. Annie Richmond; the impromptu verses "Elizabeth" and "An Acrostic," to
his cousin Elizabeth Herring, and the recently discovered valentine "To Miss Louise Olivia Hunter."
In two of the crudest of his poems he vents his spleen
against two of his contemporaries, — against Henry
T. Tuckerman in "An Enigma" [2] and against Lieu-
tenant Joseph Locke in "A West Point Lampoon."

But no student of Poe can fail to recognize in

---

[1] Here also might be mentioned his punning "Impromptu. To Kate
Carol," which Mr. J. H. Whitty has shown to have reference to Mrs. Osgood, and the two poems, "The Divine Right of Kings" and "Stanzas,"
which Mr. Whitty believes were also inspired by Poe's admiration for
Mrs. Osgood. I should not omit to mention, too, the very romantic account of a call on Mrs. Whitman in Providence which Poe vaguely describes in his later lines "To Helen."

[2] In the phrase *tuckermanities.*

"Annabel Lee" a lament for the death of Virginia Clemm, nor will he overlook the allusion to the poet's grief in consequence of her death in that strangest of all his lyrics, "Ulalume"; [1] nor will he miss the impassioned reference to himself in the closing stanza of "Israfel." And it is difficult to escape the conclusion that a dozen of his early poems, including "Dreams," "A Dream Within a Dream," "A Dream," "Stanzas," "The Happiest Day, the Happiest Hour," "To ——" ("I heed not that my earthly lot"), and the original versions of "Romance" and "Fairy-Land," echo his own griefs and disappointments, his state of mind and his attitude to the world, during his years in Richmond and Baltimore after his return from London. [2]

[1] Whether he refers also to a new love — that is, to Mrs. Shew or to Mrs. Osgood — in this poem, as has been variously alleged, must, I fear, remain a matter of conjecture.

[2] If it be contended that the allusions to disappointed ambitions, to his wounded pride, to an unbridled will, and to joys departed that recur again and again in these poems are merely an affectation of the Byronic, one has but to look into the "Valentine Letters" to be disillusioned on the point: the parallelism both in mood and in substance is too close to be accidental.

On the other hand, we can only speculate as to how far the poet has himself in mind in the apparently personal poems, "Lenore," "The Sleeper," "To ——" ("The bowers whereat, in dreams, I see"), "Bridal Ballad," "To One in Paradise," and in the uncollected poem "Serenade." Mr. Hervey Allen holds, to be sure (see his *Israfel*, p. 134), that "To One in Paradise" refers to Miss Royster and that the scene depicted there is based in some measure on the "enchanted garden" near the house of the Roysters, in which, as he declares, the lovers frequently met. But the danger of drawing too confident conclusions from mere coincidences is well illustrated in the case of "To ——" ("I saw thee on thy bridal day"), which by several of Poe's earlier biographers had been held to involve a retrospective reference to Miss Royster's marriage to Mr. Shelton,

There is every reason to believe that in "Al Aaraaf" Poe records his own faith in the divine nature of beauty, a conviction that he was later to set forth with fine earnestness in the best-known of his critical essays, "The Poetic Principle." In "Al Aaraaf" also, and likewise in his "Sonnet. To Science," he declares, in accordance with views that he expresses elsewhere,[1] his belief that knowledge is sometimes a hindrance to mortals, and, in the second of these poems, that poetry and science are in some ways incompatible. We may be equally sure that "Israfel," in its central thesis that the poet should sing from his heart, also voices his own conviction; [2] and that "Romance" in like manner expresses the poet's abiding fealty to the romantic spirit. Whether we may read out of "The Haunted Palace" a confession of the poet's belief that his own mind was at times unhinged, seems to me very questionable. But there can be little doubt that the poem reflects, though in all likelihood by an unconscious reflection, the poet's own faith in his intellectual powers and in the acuteness of his sensibilities. There is at the end of the abysmally obscure lines entitled "Stanzas" a

whereas, as we now know, the marriage did not take place until after the publication of this poem (see Ingram, p. 43; Harrison, *Poe's Works*, VII, 147; and Whitty, *The Complete Poems of Poe*, London, 1920, p. xxviii).

[1] See, for instance, "Al Aaraaf," Pt. II, ll. 163 f., and "The Colloquy of Monos and Una" (*Poe's Works*, IV, 202).

[2] Of like tenor is the second stanza of the final version of "Romance"; and see also his endorsement of this sentiment in his comment on Whitman's "Art Singing and Heart Singing" in the *Broadway Journal*, November 29, 1845 (*Whitman's Uncollected Poetry and Prose*, ed. Holloway, I, 104 f.), and in the closing lines of "Romance."

passage which may, I think, be interpreted as involving an acknowledgment by the poet of his own sense
of imperfection in the eyes of his Maker, and likewise
an expression of his faith in a Supreme Being.[1] In
the same poem we have his most explicit reference to
a trance experience of his youth, to which he attaches
supernatural significance. In "The Happiest Day,
the Happiest Hour" we seem to have a reference to
the possibility of his being succeeded by some other
heir in the household of John Allan; and in one of the
rejected readings of "Romance" (text of 1831) he
boldly declares his intention to make of himself a
poet that the world must reckon with.[2]

Other poems that appear to shadow forth in some
degree his own life are "Bridal Ballad," in which we
seem to have a reference to Miss Royster's rejection
of the poet in favor of a wealthier suitor; "Tamerlane," which may plausibly be held to refer to his
disappointment as a claimant for the hand of Miss
Royster; and *Politian*, in which, it has been suggested, he utters through certain of his characters
his own sentiments.[3] But that any of these poems
are in reality autobiographical I do not feel certain.
At best, one can only say that circumstantial evidence favors the assumption that they are.

[1] In his "Sonnet. Silence" we possibly have a very vague echo of his
belief in the after-life, and so also, possibly, in the opening lines of "For
Annie."

[2] See in this connection his letter of December 22, 1828, to John Allan
(the "Valentine Letters," pp. 88–89), in which he asserts that "the world
shall be [his] theatre" and that the time shall come when his foster-father
will not be ashamed to own him as his son.   [3] Ingram, pp. 91 f.

III

The autobiographical elements in Poe's tales and sketches, some seventy of which have been preserved, are, on the other hand, both more extensive and more readily apparent than in his poems.[1] The most tangible piece of self-revelation that appears in his stories is to be found in his "William Wilson," in which he describes under the guise of fiction, and not without fictitious detail and other bits of legitimate mystification,[2] his school-life at Stoke Newington. The building which he associates with the Manor-House School at Stoke Newington is, in reality, so his English biographer Ingram informs us,[3] not actually that of the school in which Poe studied as a boy, but that of a more manorial structure which stood on the opposite side of the street. But it appears that the poet gives a faithful description of the headmaster, the Rev. John Bransby, whom he mentions by name; he also identifies himself with his hero, to whom he ascribes the same date of birth as his own, at least in so far as day and month are concerned; and he reproduces faithfully, so Ingram assures us, the atmosphere of the town of Stoke

---

[1] In *Poe's Works*, edited by the late James A. Harrison, they comprise five volumes.

[2] He asserts, for instance, that he spent five years — "the third lustrum" — of his life at Stoke Newington, whereas we know that he spent upward of a year of his five years in England at the school of the Misses Dubourg in London (see the *Dial* for February 17, 1916, p. 144).

[3] Ingram, p. 12.

Newington, — that of a "misty-looking village" and "a dream-like and spirit-soothing place."[1]

Other stories in which Poe makes use of information drawn from his own experience or from personal observation are "The Gold-Bug," "The Balloon Hoax," "The Oblong Box," "A Tale of the Ragged Mountains," and "The Elk." In "The Gold-Bug" and "The Balloon Hoax" he introduces reminiscences of his stay at Sullivan's Island and in Charleston while a soldier in the United States army, and in "The Oblong Box" he makes use of information obtained during the same period concerning points along the coast of the Carolinas. In "A Tale of the Ragged Mountains" he evidently makes use of knowledge that he acquired while a student at the University of Virginia in 1826. It is safe to assume, too, that the particulars he gives in "The Premature Burial" concerning a hunting expedition on the James River involve a reminiscence of some similar experience in his boyhood. In "The Elk" he apparently draws on recollections of a pleasure-jaunt into the country around Philadelphia. In "Why the Little Frenchman Wears his Hand in a Sling" he gives as the address of his hero "39 Southampton Row," the same as that of John Allan and his family during the latter half of their stay in London (1815–1820). Autobiographical also must be his facetious references to the Bowling Green Fountain in "Some

[1] Ingram, p. 11.

Words with a Mummy," [1] and his mention of Earl's Hotel, Providence, in "Von Kempelen and his Discovery." [2] Mr. Hervey Allen plausibly suggests that "The Man of the Crowd" is based in part on recollections of scenes that Poe became familiar with during his stay in London; [3] and the same is probably true of certain scenes in "King Pest," — in particular, the reference to St. Andrew's Stair, which was not far from John Allan's place of business, 18 Basinghall Street. Indirectly also "Ligeia" must be accounted autobiographical, if we may credit an autograph note by the poet (in one of the printed texts of the story) to the effect that the tale originated in a dream. [4]

In other stories — and here again we can be very sure of our ground — Poe gives expression, either in proper person or through some one of his characters, to his own prejudices and dislikes. Thus in "Never Bet the Devil Your Head" and "Some Words with a Mummy" he expresses his contempt for the Transcendentalists and his dislike of the *Dial*; in "Never Bet the Devil Your Head" he speaks with disdain of Emerson and Carlyle; [5] in a late revision of his farce, "The Duc de L'Omelette," he refers contemptuously to the city of Boston, [6] as he does

[1] *Poe's Works*, VI, 134. See *Doings of Gotham*, ed. Spannuth and Mabbott, p. 26, for his characterization of the Bowling Green Fountain as an absurdity.

[2] According to Woodberry (II, 284) he was a guest at Earl's Hotel late in 1848.

[3] *Israfel*, p. 479.   [4] Ingram, p. 126.
[5] *Poe's Works*, IV, 218.   [6] *Ibid.*, II, 199.

again and again in his miscellaneous prose; and in several of his tales he expresses disapproval of Bentham and the Utilitarians,[1] of the "perfectionists" or "perfectibilians," [2] and of uplift movements generally.[3] In the introduction of his "Never Bet the Devil Your Head," to which he ironically gives the sub-title "A Moral Tale," he records — ironically again — his dislike of a tale with a moral, observing in the same connection that the charge had been brought against him that he had never written a moral tale. There is animus in his references to Rufus W. Griswold and Henry T. Tuckerman in the opening paragraph of "The Angel of the Odd"; [4] and in his mention of "Clarke on Tongue" and "Prentice's Billingsgate" in "The Literary Life of Thingum Bob, Esq." [5] he indulges in a backhanded slap at Lewis Gaylord Clark and George Denison Prentice.[6] In other stories he airs his dislike of certain contemporary magazines, — of *Blackwood's* in "How to Write a Blackwood Article" and

---

[1] *Poe's Works*, IV, 201; VI, 204.

[2] *Ibid.*, II, 38.

[3] See in particular "The Colloquy of Monos and Una" and "The Elk," in which he deplores the rise of industrialism in America; and see also *Doings of Gotham*, p. 25.

[4] *Poe's Works*, VI, 103.

[5] *Ibid.*, p. 21. See, too, the mention of "Hewitt's Seraphic . . . Oil of Archangels" in a rejected reading of "Loss of Breath" (II, 357), in which he makes a thrust at John H. Hewitt, who had been awarded by the Baltimore *Saturday Visiter* a prize that had been first voted to Poe for "The Coliseum."

[6] See also his reference to J. T. Buckingham and his mention of "the odious old woods of Concord" in "X-ing a Paragrab" (*Poe's Works*, VI, 232, 233).

"A Predicament" and in the sub-title of "Loss of Breath"; [1] of the *North American Review* (which he speaks of as the "North American Quarterly Hum Drum")[2] in "The Literary Life of Thingum Bob, Esq."; and possibly, also, of the *Knickerbocker* in his mention of the "Lollipop" in the same story.

So also it is reasonable to assume that he reveals his own convictions when he satirizes in "Mystification" the ante-bellum custom of duelling, and when he pokes fun at puffery and excessive laudation of whatever sort in "Lionizing," at literary affectation and sham in "How to Write a Blackwood Article" and "A Predicament," and at fraud of various sorts in "The Business Man" and "Diddling Considered as One of the Exact Sciences," and at the "tale with a moral" in "Never Bet the Devil Your Head." I suspect that he airs one of his own prejudices in his ridicule of system in the earlier paragraphs of "The Business Man" (originally entitled "Peter Pendulum"), in which he perhaps had in mind the ways and habits of his foster-father. And it is highly probable that in "Mellonta Tauta" he echoes his own impatience with insincerity and show in religion in his reference (such as Emerson might have made) to the church of his day as standing for the worship of "Wealth and Fashion," [3] and he is but voicing his own dislike of arrogance and brag in the later paragraphs of "Some Words with a Mummy," [4] and of

[1] "A Tale Neither In Nor Out of Blackwood."
[2] *Poe's Works*, VI, 5. [3] *Ibid.*, pp. 212 f. [4] *Ibid.*, pp. 133 f.

the bustle as an article of feminine adornment — to mingle great things with small — in his humorous allusions to that article of dress in "The Thousand-and-Second Tale of Scheherazade" and elsewhere.[1]

In yet other stories he records in one capacity or another sentiments which we know to have been his own. In "The Murders in the Rue Morgue," for instance, he asserts that "the *truly* imaginative are never otherwise than analytic";[2] and later in the same story that "by undue profundity we perplex and enfeeble thought."[3] In "The Mystery of Marie Rogêt" he remarks that "a true philosophy will always show that a vast, perhaps the larger portion of truth, arises from the seemingly irrelevant";[4] and in "Mellonta Tauta" that "the true and only true thinkers" are "men of ardent imagination."[5] He utters his own convictions, in all likelihood, when he asserts in "The Black Cat" that "perverseness is one of the primitive impulses of the human heart";[6] when he remarks in "Metzengerstein," in true Frostian phrase, that "near neighbors are seldom friends";[7]

[1] *Poe's Works*, v, 206; vi, 101, 213.

[2] *Ibid.*, iv, 150.

[3] *Ibid.*, p. 166. Cf. also a rejected variant of "Hans Pfaall" (ii, 332), in which he raises the question whether "profundity itself might not, in matters of a purely speculative nature, be detected as a legitimate source of falsity and error"; and see his statement in the "Letter to B——" (vii, xxxix) that Coleridge erred by reason of his profundity.

[4] *Ibid.*, v, 39; *Doings of Gotham*, ed. Spannuth and Mabbott, p. 66.

[5] *Poe's Works*, vi, 206. The statement was made, in all likelihood, with himself in mind.

[6] *Ibid.*, v, 146.   [7] *Ibid.*, ii, 186.

when he observes in "The Assignation" that "in the manner of the true gentleman, we are always aware of a difference from the bearing of the vulgar, without being . . . able to determine in what such difference consists"; [1] when he declares in "The Elk" that the "finest landscapes" in America are to be "reached only by bypaths"; [2] and when he maintains in "The Domain of Arnheim," in the person of his hero, that "the four elementary . . . conditions of bliss" are "free exercise in the open air," "love of woman," "contempt of ambition," and "an object of unceasing pursuit." [3]

In a good many of his stories he depicts himself or reflects some side of his personality either in his hero or in his heroine. "Roderick Usher" in "The Fall of the House of Usher" supplies the most obvious illustration; [4] but "Ligeia" in the story of that title affords an almost equally obvious example. "Morella" and "Hans Pfaall" and the artist in "The Assignation" are other examples. Apparently he had himself in mind and his own youthful escapades in "The Spectacles" in the passage: "I touched upon my college indiscretions — upon my extravagances — upon my carousals — upon my debts — upon my flirtations," [5] and probably also in "Berenice" when he writes:

---

[1] *Ibid.*, p. 119.   [2] *Ibid.*, v, 158.

[3] *Ibid.*, vi, 177. — See for other passages in which he probably speaks in proper person, *ibid.*, ii, 154; v, 69, 298; vi, 43.

[4] Mr. Hervey Allen (*Israfel*, p. 445) characterizes the picture that Poe gives of "Roderick Usher" as the "most perfect pen-portrait of Poe himself which is known."   [5] *Poe's Works*, v, 198.

"I loitered away my boyhood in books, and dissipated my youth in reverie." [1] In still other stories he pictures his hero (or heroine) as having, like himself, a high (or wide) forehead.[2]

There is, too, the very intangible but none the less significant revelation of Poe's own interests and predilections: of his interest in secret writing, for example, as it comes out in "The Gold-Bug," and in ratiocination as exhibited in the detective stories,[3] his fondness for metaphysical speculations as revealed in "Bon-Bon," "Morella," "Mesmeric Revelation," and "The Power of Words," and his curiosity about scientific discovery as reflected in "The Thousand-and-Second Tale of Scheherazade," "Some Words with a Mummy," and "Mellonta Tauta," as also in his stories about ballooning and in his tales that deal with mesmerism and phrenology. His native propensity for mystification and hoaxing comes out in the tale entitled "Mystification," in "The Balloon Hoax," and in "Hans Pfaall." There is, I dare say, a reflection of the man's nature also in his display of learning in certain of the stories, at least in so far as such pedantic display was not deliberately indulged in for purposes of satire or for the sake of atmosphere. And in the sardonic nature of Poe's humor there must also be a reflection of one side of the man.

[1] *Poe's Works*, ii, 17.
[2] *Ibid.*, pp. 23, 32, 134, 174, 250; iii, 279; iv, 103, 281; v, 163.
[3] Both "Dupin," then, and the "Minister D——" in "The Purloined Letter" are adumbrations of the poet.

Among stories that are less surely autobiographical but that may not improbably be so interpreted are "Three Sundays in a Week," which apparently affords a reminiscence of the opposition on the part of John Allan to Poe's marriage with Miss Royster; "The Business Man," in which we have a farcical characterization of a "weak-minded"[1] old gentleman who placed his son at the age of fifteen in "the counting-house of what he termed 'a respectable hardware and commission merchant doing a capital bit of business'" — in consequence of which he presently ran away from home;[2] and *Arthur Gordon Pym,* which in its opening paragraphs seems to echo some of the incidents of Poe's life in Richmond in his boyhood.[3] There is the possibility, also, that his mention of the cousin relationship existing between hero and heroine in "Berenice" and "Eleonora" and "Three Sundays in a Week" is of autobiographical import, though the first of those stories must have been written in the early stages of his courtship of his cousin.[4]

[1] *Poe's Works,* IV, 123. Poe uses the same epithet in characterizing the father of William Wilson in the story of that title (*ibid.,* III, 300).

[2] *Ibid.,* IV, 124. It may very well be that the bill drawn up in clerk-like fashion in "The Business Man" (pp. 125 f.) and his mention of day-book, ledger, and journal reflect the experience, slight though it must have been, obtained by Poe in the counting-house of Ellis and Allan in the twenties.

[3] Augustus Barnard in the same story seems to be a reflection of Ebenezer Burling, one of Poe's chums during his early years in Richmond.

[4] And shall I expose myself to the charge of dallying with false surmise if I suggest that Poe's reference to gin as a fiend in "The Man of the Crowd" (*Poe's Works,* IV, 144) and his exclamation, "For what disease

I shall do no more than mention here that in "A Tale of Jerusalem" and "Four Beasts in One," in various quotations and allusions scattered through his stories, and very explicitly in the style of his sketches "Shadow" and "Silence," we have evidence of Poe's acquaintance with the Scriptures; and that the color and the glamor of style that distinguish some of his stories are possibly a reflection of the Southern environment in which he grew up. There are, too, in his stories passages that suggest dissatisfaction on his part with the workings of democracy in America, though they do not, I think, indicate that he was entirely out of sympathy with a republican form of government.[1]

It may be, too, that his references in several of his stories to morphine and laudanum and their effects grew out of his own experience with narcotics;[2] and

is like Alcohol!" in "The Black Cat" (*ibid.*, v, 145) actually represent his convictions, however inconsistent this may seem with his conduct? In a letter published in the *Columbia Spy* in 1844 (*Doings of Gotham*, p. 39) he characterizes saloons as "hot-houses of iniquity," and asserts that "no one can entertain a doubt" as to "the direct benefits accruing" from the closing of the saloon.

[1] See, for instance, *Poe's Works*, IV, 203; VI, 136, 208. On the other hand, it should be noted that he remarks in "Hop-Frog" (*ibid.*, VI, 217) that "days are rather longer at court than elsewhere"; and that he takes Fanny Kemble to task in a review of her *Journal* (*ibid.*, VIII, 28 f.) for her animadversions on the workings of a democracy in America, remarking on his part that the laboring man is infinitely better off in a democracy than in a monarchy.

[2] See in particular a discarded passage with which "The Oval Portrait" originally opened (*ibid.*, IV, 316 f.).

So, too, Professor Woodberry suggests (*America in Literature*, p. 148) that Poe reveals in his stories something of cruelty in his make-up (he mentions "The Black Cat" and "The Pit and the Pendulum" as ex-

Mr. Brownell holds that we have in certain of his stories evidence of the effects upon him of inebriety.[1]

In a still more remote sense we have a revelation of self in Poe's references to persons that he knew, — to Mrs. Annie Richmond ("Annie") in "Landor's Cottage," to "Cornelius Wyatt"[2] in "The Oblong Box,"[3] and to John Randolph of Roanoke in "The Strange Case of M. Valdemar," — and in certain names that he adopts for characters introduced into this or that story, as "Dubourg" (the name of his school-mistresses while he was a student in London in 1816–1817) in "The Mystery of Marie Rogêt," and Andrew Thornton and Alexander Wormley, names of prominent families in Virginia with whom he was acquainted, in his "Julius Rodman." The name

amples); but I am not sure that this is a safe inference to draw from the fact that Poe frequently depicts scenes of frightful cruelty in his stories. It seems to me probable, as Dr. Napier Wilt has pointed out (*Modern Philology*, xxv, 102), that Poe was but catering to a contemporary demand and following a fashion set by inferior tale-writers of his day. It may be noted in this connection that Poe in his review of Longstreet's *Georgia Scenes* (*Poe's Works*, viii, 262 f.) calls attention to and deplores the display of cruelty in certain rural sections of the ante-bellum South, specifically in the barbarous practice of "gander-pulling," and that he also takes occasion in a late review (*ibid.*, xii, 248) to complain of the excess of the horrible in the novels of William Gilmore Simms.

[1] *American Prose Masters*, p. 230.

[2] He had collaborated with Professor Thomas Wyatt in the compilation of their treatise on conchology.

[3] Is it possible that in "Wertemuller" in a cancelled passage in "Mystification" (*Poe's Works*, iv, 279) Poe has reference to William Wertenbaker, who was librarian of the University of Virginia during the year that he spent as a student there? And may it be that in his statement in the same story, "I have seen the protector, the consul . . . aghast at the convolutions of a weathercock," he has reference to Thomas Jefferson and his well-known interest in mechanical invention?

"William Wilson" may also have been suggested in like manner by a name that he had probably heard his foster-father use, for it appears from the Ellis-Allan Papers that Allan had dealings with two merchants bearing that name, one a Quaker living at Kendal and the other a Virginian who was an agent for Washington College.

IV

There is, I dare say, a good deal more of autobiography in Poe's poems and tales than I have been able to discover. More light will doubtless be thrown on the matter with the revelation of new facts about Poe's life and about his habits of composition. But enough evidence of a positive nature has already been brought forward to demonstrate beyond any question that the poet, however objective he may appear to be in his imaginative writings, drew extensively on his own life for the materials underlying his art. In the case of the poems the body of self-revelatory material, though small in compass, is, in reality, comparatively large: it involves in some way virtually half of Poe's poems; and though it is, for the most part, vague and cloudlike, this was entirely in keeping with the poet's theory that the lyric should hide its meaning under a cloak of "indefiniteness." And in the stories the revelation of self is both abundant and, much of the way, readily evident.

THE ORIGINS OF POE

I

A GOOD deal has already been done by way of revealing Poe's sources. Even before his death something had been accomplished in this direction, and other suggestions were forthcoming shortly after his death. "Outis," for instance, in 1845, in the unhappy "Longfellow War," called attention to the similarity between Poe's use of the repetend in "The Raven" and Coleridge's use of that device in "The Ancient Mariner." [1] In the following year an anonymous contributor to the Philadelphia *Saturday Evening Post* [2] disclosed the fact that Poe had drawn freely on Captain Thomas Brown's *Textbook of Conchology* (1833) for his *Conchologist's First Book* (1839), a compilation to which in an evil hour he had attached his name. In 1848 Henry B. Hirst, one-time friend of the poet, pointed out, in an article in the Philadelphia *Saturday Courier*, that Poe had apparently found the "leading idea" of his "Ulalume" in a poem of Thomas B. Read's. [3] During the year follow-

[1] *Poe's Works*, XII, 50 f. "Outis" made light of this, to be sure, but the poet Stedman, years later, expressed the opinion (*Poe's Works*, ed. Stedman and Woodberry, X, xxvi) that Poe "surely found his clew" in Coleridge's poem.   [2] In its issue of March 14, 1846.
[3] The Philadelphia *Saturday Courier*, January 22, 1848.

[147]

ing Poe's death Lewis Gaylord Clark, in the *Knicker-bocker*, charged Poe with having borrowed materials for "The Pit and the Pendulum" from a tale in *Blackwood's*.[1] And in 1857 a writer in the *Southern Literary Messenger* noted some of the resemblances between "The Raven" and Mrs. Browning's "Lady Geraldine's Courtship."[2] But it was not until the publication of the biographies of Poe by Ingram and Woodberry — in 1880 and 1885, respectively — that any serious or systematic attempt was made towards laying bare Poe's sources. Each of these eminent authorities on the poet's life brought out a good deal of important information about the sources on which Poe drew; and it is to them most of all that we are indebted for such information as we have concerning his literary borrowings, although scarcely a year has passed since the beginning of the century that has not revealed additional evidence as to his origins.

In the present essay I shall attempt to bring together the suggestions that have been made (of a seemingly valid nature) with regard to the poet's origins;[3] to which I shall add certain suggestions of my own; and on the basis of this assembled evidence I shall venture sundry generalizations as to the nature and extent of Poe's indebtednesses and as to his methods of working with his originals.

[1] The *Knickerbocker*, xxxv, 163 (February, 1850).

[2] The *Southern Literary Messenger*, xxv, 334–335 (November, 1857).

[3] In foot-notes I have endeavored to make acknowledgment of all specific suggestions that I have availed myself of.

In my discussion of Poe's backgrounds,[1] I have already touched on one side of the subject. As I endeavored to show there, Poe owed a good deal to his age and to the land in which he lived and wrote. I have also anticipated the subject in a measure in my discussion above of the use made by Poe of his own experiences and observations in his poems and tales.[2] In considering his origins it will be impossible to ignore entirely these aspects of the subject; but I shall concern myself here mainly with Poe's literary origins, — with his indebtedness to books and the printed page. I shall take up in order his poems, his tales, and his critical and miscellaneous essays.

II

In any discussion of the origins of Poe's poems the observation is inevitable at the outset that Poe was a product of the Romantic Movement, a scion of the same stock that gave to us Byron and Shelley and Moore and Coleridge. As with them, so with Poe, the emphasis was largely upon the subjective, the remote, the unusual, the ideal. Here and there, too, especially in his later poems, there was a strain of sentimentality; and in several of the earlier poems — in "Tamerlane" and "Al Aaraaf" and "Israfel" — he dealt with Oriental materials.

It was to the Romantics, moreover, — and in particular to Byron and Moore and Coleridge,— that

[1] *Supra*, pp. 99 f.   [2] Pp. 126 f.

Poe looked, in so far as he looked beyond his own experiences and observation, for the materials out of which he was to fabricate his scant half a hundred lyrics; and to them also he turned for models and for inspiration.[1]

His most substantial obligations as poet were to Lord Byron. The longest of his early poems, "Tamerlane," was evidently written in imitation of *The Giaour*, which it patterns after both in matter and in style.[2] The death-bed confession to a priest, with which the poem opens, seems also to have owed something to the parallel situation in the third act of *Manfred*, in which, as in Poe's poem, the dying hero declines the absolution offered him by a priest. The influence of the anacoluthic style of Byron's verse-tales is also discoverable in "Tamerlane"; and there are echoes of other poems of Byron, especially of *Childe Harold*, from which the words "sound of revelry by night" are introduced *verbatim* into the earliest printed text of the poem.

But even more obvious than the debt to *Manfred* and *The Giaour* that appears in "Tamerlane" is the borrowing from Byron seen in his early lyric "Spirits of the Dead," which is, much of the way, a mosaic of materials drawn from the incantation at the end of the first scene of *Manfred*. The two lines,

---

[1] The nature of these indebtednesses I have tried to bring out in detail in my edition of *Poe's Poems* (Boston, 1917). I shall here do little more than mention the chief influences and borrowings.

[2] See *Poe's Works*, ed. Stedman and Woodberry, x, xx.

Now are thoughts thou shalt not banish,
Now are visions ne'er to vanish,

manifestly go back to Byron's lines,

There are shades which will not vanish,
There are thoughts thou canst not banish.

The opening lines of Poe's poem as first published in 1827,

Thy soul shall find itself alone,
Alone of all on earth — unknown,

seem likewise to hark back to another couplet in the same lyric,

By a power to thee unknown,
Thou canst never be alone;

and there are yet other verbal parallels that can hardly be accidental.

Byron's influence is also to be detected in "Stanzas," which takes its cue from a stanza of *The Island* (used as the motto of the poem); in "A Dream Within a Dream" (originally entitled "Imitation," in acknowledgment, I take it, of an indebtedness to Byron's "The Dream"); and in "Romance," which was not improbably written, as Professor C. Alphonso Smith once suggested,[1] by way of protest against Byron's lines "To Romance," in which the English bard professes, in a fit of caprice, to abjure Romance as a guide.

[1] *Modern Language Notes*, xxxiii, 174 (March, 1918).

In a pathetic letter to his foster-father written from Fortress Monroe on May 29, 1829, Poe declared that he had long since "given up Byron as a model"; [1] but the influence of Byron may, nevertheless, be traced also in the volumes of 1829 and 1831 and in still later poems. "The City in the Sea," for example, seems to have found the suggestion of a number of its details in Byron's fragment entitled "Darkness." It is reasonable to assume that "The Coliseum" owes something to the famous description of the Roman amphitheatre in *Childe Harold*; and Mr. Paul Elmer More has suggested that the refrain "nevermore" in "The Raven" is to be traced to Byron's use of it in *Don Juan*. [2]

To Thomas Moore, also, Poe's debt was not inconsiderable. It may be clearly seen in the volume of 1827 in the lyric "Evening Star," which was unmistakably based on Moore's lyric "While Gazing on the Moon's Light." Poe, in a foot-note, confessed, moreover, to an indebtedness to Moore in his "Fairy-Land" (1829). The most obvious of his borrowings from the Irish lyrist appears, however, in the long poem "Al Aaraaf." The catalogue of flowers near the beginning of that poem is largely drawn, as Professor Woodberry pointed out a good many years ago,[3] from *Lalla Rookh*, some passages being taken

[1] The "Valentine Letters," p. 134.
[2] *Studies in Philology*, xx, 306 (July, 1923). It should be noted, however, that Shelley had used the same refrain in his lines entitled "A Lament," and that Lowell had also used it in his "Threnodia" (1839).
[3] *Poe's Works*, ed. Stedman and Woodberry, x, 223.

from the body of Moore's poem and others from Moore's notes. I shall cite two instances. Poe writes of the Nelumbo:

> And the Nelumbo bud that floats forever
> With Indian Cupid down the holy river.

Moore had written in a foot-note: "The Indians feign that Cupid was first seen floating down the Ganges on the Nymphaea Nelumbo." Of the Sephalica Poe writes:

> The Sephalica, budding with young bees,
> Uprear'd its purple stem around her knees.

Moore had written in *Lalla Rookh*:

> Of falling waters lulling as the song
> Of Indian bees at sunset, when they throng
> Around the fragrant Nilica, and deep
> In its blue blossoms hum themselves to sleep;

and in a foot-note had explained that the Nilica is the same as the Sephalica.

The debt to Coleridge, on the other hand, though of much more significance than the debt to Byron or to Moore, — for it affected mainly the poems of Poe's riper years, and involves in no small measure his poetical creed, — was largely unsubstantial. The only very close approximation to Coleridge that I find in Poe's poems appears in a much-discussed line in the earlier "To Helen,"

> Like those Nicean barks of yore,

which clearly resembles Coleridge's line in "Youth and Age,"

> Like those trim skiffs, unknown of yore.

But it was to Coleridge, most of all, that Poe was obligated for his theory of verse, the *Biographia Literaria* prompting his theorizing on poetics as did no other book or group of books.[1] He was almost certainly influenced by Coleridge, moreover, in the music and diction of some of his best verse. In particular, the mood and style of "Kubla Khan" seem to be reflected in "The City in the Sea"; there are lines in "The Sleeper" that suggest passages in "Christabel"; and it is altogether plausible that the melody of "The Raven" owed something to the internal rhyme and the repetends in "The Ancient Mariner."

There were debts also to Keats and Shelley. The immediate impulse to the writing of the "Sonnet. To Science" Poe probably owed to Keats's "Lamia," in particular to the famous passage (ll. 229–238) concerning the baleful effects of "cold philosophy" upon beauty and the imagination; and a parallel scarcely less striking exists between the closing lines of Poe's sonnet,

> Hast thou not dragged Diana from her car,
>   And driven the Hamadryad from the wood
>   To seek a shelter in some happier star?

[1] See Floyd Stovall, "Poe's Debt to Coleridge," University of Texas *Studies in English*, No. 10, pp. 70 f. (1930).

> Hast thou not torn the Naiad from her flood,
> The Elfin from the green grass, and from me
> The summer dream beneath the tamarind tree?

and the lines near the beginning of "Lamia":

> Upon a time, before the faery broods
> Drove Nymph and Satyr from the prosperous woods,
> Before king Oberon's bright diadem,
> Sceptre, and mantle, clasp'd with dewy gem,
> Frighted away the Dryads and the Fauns
> From rushes green, and brakes, and cowslip'd lawns.

To Shelley, Poe's debt was, as in the case of his debt to Coleridge, largely a matter of atmosphere and mood rather than of phrasal echo or appropriation. In particular, I find the Shelleyan ideality in "Israfel" and in the songs in "Al Aaraaf"; and there are passages also in the Shelleyan manner in "Dream-Land," in "To One in Paradise," and in the "Sonnet. Silence."

Here and there, too, one may catch echoes of certain of Wordsworth's lines, despite the fact that Poe more than once recorded his disapproval both of Wordsworth's theory of verse and of his practice. The lines from "The Valley of Unrest," for example,

> That palpitate like the chill seas
> Around the misty Hebrides,

although conventional, probably owed something to Wordsworth's memorable lines in "The Solitary Reaper,"

> Breaking the silence of the seas
> Among the farthest Hebrides.

The line,

> Gone are the glory and the gloom,

in the 1831 text of "Romance," is perhaps an echo of a couplet from the "Intimations Ode,"

> Whither is fled the visionary gleam?
> Where is it now, the glory and the dream?

The collocation "clouds of glory" appeared in a manuscript version of "To —— —— ——" ("Not long ago, the writer of these lines");[1] and the magic lines,

> To the glory that was Greece
> And the grandeur that was Rome,

resemble a line from Wordsworth's "Stanzas: Composed in the Simplon Pass" (1822):

> The beauty of Florence, and the grandeur of Rome.[2]

The indebtedness of "The Raven" to Mrs. Browning's "Lady Geraldine's Courtship" (1844) is readily obvious. It appears most plainly in the line (13),

And the silken, sad, uncertain rustling of each purple
curtain,

---

[1] See *Poe's Works*, ed. Stedman and Woodberry, x, 194–195.

[2] Poe's lines originally read,

> "To the beauty of fair Greece,
> To the grandeur of old Rome,"

which approximates Wordsworth's line even more closely. — See for other possible indebtednesses to Wordsworth, H. M. Belden's *Observation and Imagination in Coleridge and Poe*, pp. 30, 36.

which surely had its origin in Mrs. Browning's line (381),

With a murmurous stir uncertain, in the air the purple curtain.

It appears also in the line (43),

Then this ebony bird beguiling my sad fancy into smiling,

which goes back evidently to the line (389),

Ever, evermore the while in a slow silence she kept smiling,

and also, apparently, in the line (87),

Desolate yet all undaunted, on this desert land enchanted,

which resembles Mrs. Browning's line (380),

O'er the desolate sand-desert of my heart and life undone.

There is an unmistakable similarity to Mrs. Browning's poem, also, in the metrical movement and in the use of internal rhyme.[1]

[1] Poe had reviewed Mrs. Browning's volume (*The Drama of Exile, and Other Poems*) containing "Lady Geraldine's Courtship" in the *Broadway Journal* of January 4 and 11, 1845 (*Poe's Works*, XII, 1 f.), and had in the course of his review remarked that with one exception he had "never perused a poem combining so much of the fiercest passion with so much of the most ethereal fancy, as the 'Lady Geraldine's Courtship'" (*ibid.*, p. 16), and in the same connection he had quoted (*ibid.*, p. 18) from Mrs. Browning's poem the stanza containing the last of her lines cited above. Among other passages quoted in his review (*ibid.*, p. 30) is the stanza from Mrs. Browning's "The Lost Bower," beginning:

"So, young muser, I sat listening
To my Fancy's wildest word:
On a sudden, through the glistening
Leaves around, a little stirred,
Came a sound, a sense of music which was rather felt than heard,"

The idea of the raven, a talking bird, was with almost equal certainty suggested by Dickens's *Barnaby Rudge* (1841), which Poe had reviewed in *Graham's Magazine* for February, 1842,[1] remarking at the time that Dickens's raven could have been more effectively used if conceived of as symbolical, the croakings of the bird being heard "prophetically . . . in the course of the drama," what (as he tells us in his "Philosophy of Composition") is precisely Poe's conception in "The Raven."

Hood's sonnet on "Silence" evidently suggested to Poe his sonnet on the same subject. The two poems possess a good deal in common, though Poe gives to his a different twist. That Poe knew Hood's "Silence" is proved only too convincingly, moreover, by his reproduction of it above his own initial (whether maliciously or for purposes of mystification we cannot be certain) in *Burton's Gentleman's Magazine* six months before he published there his own sonnet.[2]

Reminiscences of Milton appear in the second part of "Al Aaraaf," particularly in the description of Nesace's temple. The basic idea of "Israfel" seems to have been suggested by two lines from Béranger's "Le Refus" (1830),

> Son cœur est un luth suspendu;
> Sitôt qu'on le touche, il résonne, —

which will, I think, also remind one of "The Raven," and certainly of its rhythmical movement.   [1] *Poe's Works*, XI, 63.
    [2] *Burton's Gentleman's Magazine*, v, 144 (September, 1839).

lines that Poe later used as a motto for "The Fall of
the House of Usher." His "Enigma" was apparently
suggested by a sonnet of Lope de Vega. And a col-
league of mine, Professor Robert A. Law, has called
attention to a very probable source of "Annabel
Lee" in a poem "The Mourner," published in the
Charleston *Courier* in 1807.[1]

For the rest it is clear that certain ideas for the
setting in "Al Aaraaf" came from the Koran, and
that both "The City in the Sea" and "The Valley
of Unrest" owe something to the Bible. "El Dorado"
was confessedly prompted by the California gold
rush of 1849; and *Politian* is a reworking of the newspaper accounts of a murder that took place in Kentucky in the 1820's.[2]

There is also a good deal of autobiography in Poe's
poems, as I have endeavored to show in another essay
in this volume.[3] Aside from the reflections of the
poet's mind and personality, there are several specific references to incidents in his life (as in his
sonnet "To My Mother"), there are adumbrations,
apparently, of still other incidents in his life (notably
in "Tamerlane"), and there are echoes of his opinions and thinking on philosophical and other problems (as in "Al Aaraaf" and "Israfel").

With respect to Poe's methods of working with
his source materials, we have a confession unparal-
leled, so far as I know, for its circumstantiality in

[1] *Journal of English and Germanic Philology*, XXI, 341 f. (April, 1922).
[2] See Poe's *Politian*, ed. Mabbott, Richmond, 1923, pp. 51 f.
[3] *Supra*, pp. 131 f.

his "Philosophy of Composition," an essay in which he professes to tell in detail of the processes through which "The Raven" passed in the course of its composition. There is, I imagine, more of truth in Poe's account than the average reader would at first be disposed to concede. But at least Poe does not tell the whole truth, for he makes no mention of his borrowings from Mrs. Browning and from Dickens,[1] and he ignores the fact that he had, long before writing "The Raven," dealt with a similar situation in other poems, — notably in his "Lenore," — and also in some of the tales. But even though we should grant, as more than one able critic has done, that Poe's account of the composition of "The Raven" is largely true, we can be virtually certain that his account does not represent his practice in the case of many of his poems, — if, indeed, of any other of his poems. That his verses grew slowly under his shaping hand is clearly indicated by the frequency with which he recast most of his lyrics and the very large number of revisions that he made, the cancelled matter exceeding in bulk in some instances the entire poem in its final form.[2]

III

In the preface of his volume of poems published in 1845, Poe declared that poetry had been with him "not a purpose, but a passion." The case was dif-

---

[1] *Supra*, pp. 156 f.

[2] His habits of revision I have discussed in the introduction of my edition of Poe's poems, pp. xxxv f.

ferent with his short stories. While he must have written some of his stories with much zest, he turned to the writing of fiction primarily, we can be sure, for the purpose of making a living. Poetry, he had found, did not pay, at least in dollars and cents: there was little market for it; and it was necessary for him to resort to something that would bring him in an income. We do not know when he served his apprenticeship with the short story. There is a tradition that he wrote some of his tales before he left the University of Virginia; but of the first of his stories to be published so far as we know — a group of five stories that appeared in the Philadelphia *Saturday Courier* in 1832 — none can be confidently traced back to that period.[1]

But there was a market for the short story, as Poe learned from his reading in current magazines. He read these closely, both English and American, and he not only discovered that there was a demand for the short story, but he also learned what sort of story the editors found most available. He concluded, as he tells us in a very illuminating letter written in 1835,[2] that the stories most in demand with the periodicals of the day were of four several types: those involving "the fearful colored into the horrible" (that is, the tale of terror, which was most of all in vogue); those involving "the ludicrous heightened into the grotesque"; those involving "the witty exaggerated into

[1] See the *Dial*, LX, 146 (February 17, 1916).
[2] See the article of Professor Napier Wilt, *Modern Philology*, XXV, 101 f. (August, 1927).

the burlesque"; and those involving "the singular heightened into the strange and mystical." How closely he adhered to these types, in catering to the demands of the periodicals, will be at once apparent from an examination of his early stories. "Metzengerstein," which appears to have been the first of his stories to make its way into print, very well illustrates the first of these categories, "the fearful colored into the horrible." "Loss of Breath" illustrates very effectively the second category, "the ludicrous heightened into the grotesque." "The Duc de L'Omelette" answers very well to his third category, "the witty exaggerated into the burlesque." And his "Morella," to be followed by "Ligeia" and others among his best stories, obviously serves as an example of "the singular heightened into the strange and mystical." Most of Poe's early stories and a good many of his later stories fall under one or another of these rubrics.

In this same remarkable letter Poe mentions some of the stories that had found their way into the contemporary magazines and which seemed to him to represent contemporary modes, — among them, Mudford's "The Man in the Bell," which he was presently to burlesque in "A Predicament," [1] and two of Bulwer's stories, "Monos and Daimonos" (which apparently served as a partial source of

---

[1] He drew on the same story in the composition of three other stories: "The Devil in the Belfry," "Never Bet the Devil Your Head," and "The Pit and the Pendulum."

"Silence. A Fable") and "Manuscript Found in a Madhouse" [1] (which perhaps suggested to him the title of the "MS. Found in a Bottle"). In his "How to Write a Blackwood Article" (1838) Poe makes a similar list of stories that had been published in *Blackwood's*,[2] including again "The Man in the Bell," and in addition "The Dead Alive," "The Involuntary Experimentalist," and Samuel Warren's "Passages from the Diary of a Late Physician." In each of this second group of stories, as Miss Margaret Alterton has rightly observed,[3] the emphasis is on the analysis of sensation, which furnishes accordingly a fifth type of story which Poe found to be in vogue and which he proceeded to pattern after in his own stories. For although he ridicules the analysis of sensation both in "How to Write a Blackwood Article" and in "Loss of Breath," he employed this method for his own purposes and with serious intent in his "MS. Found in a Bottle" among his earlier stories and in "The Pit and the Pendulum," "A Descent into the Maelström," and "The Colloquy of Monos and Una" among later stories.

There were many stories of these types in the magazines of the day, and not only in *Blackwood's* and other British periodicals, but also in the American periodicals, as *Godey's Lady's Book*, the *Mirror*, the *Casket*, and the *Saturday Evening Post*. Professor

[1] Both of these stories appeared in an early edition published at Boston by Phillips, Sampson, and Company.

[2] *Poe's Works*, II, 273–274.

[3] *Origins of Poe's Critical Theory*, pp. 30 f.

Woodberry informs us that W. M. Griswold believed that four stories published in *Godey's* in 1833–1834 were Poe's,[1] basing his belief on the similarity in matter and style to Poe's fully authenticated stories. Professor Wilt has called attention to upwards of a dozen other stories resembling Poe's authentic work that appeared in English and American magazines about the same time;[2] and reference to the magazines and weeklies of the thirties will reveal scores of others. It was from such stories that Poe derived the impulse to the writing of his own stories, and their significance in accounting for his origins as a writer of short stories cannot easily be overestimated.

Poe also, as I have already brought out in discussing his backgrounds, catered to the demands of his day in treating in his stories a number of specific subjects that were popular with contributors to the current periodicals, — as the pestilence and its terrors, exploration by land and sea, premature burial, and mesmerism.

Several of his stories, moreover, originated as satires on contemporary books or fashions or customs for which Poe had developed a distaste. In "How to Write a Blackwood Article" and its sequel, "A Predicament," he endeavors to satirize the type of story in favor with *Blackwood's*. "Loss of Breath," which originally bore the sub-title "A Tale Neither In Nor Out of Blackwood," is confessedly a burlesque

[1] Woodberry, I, 134 n.
[2] *Modern Philology*, xxv, 103.

on *Blackwood's.* "A Tale of Jerusalem," as Professor James Southall Wilson has shown,[1] was intended as a burlesque of Horace Smith's *Zillah, a Tale of Jerusalem* (1828). "X-ing a Paragrab" and "The Literary Life of Thingum Bob, Esq.," among later stories, have to do with the foibles of editors and with their animosities. "Lionizing" is directed against extravagance in praise of some popular hero, specifically in this instance of N. P. Willis. "Never Bet the Devil Your Head" pokes fun at the moral tale, "The Devil in the Belfry" at small-town complacency, and "The Business Man" and "Diddling Considered as One of the Exact Sciences" at various kinds of fraud and quackery.

The plots for a number of his stories Poe found in the periodicals of his time. Two very interesting examples of his reliance upon contemporary newspapers are afforded by "The Mystery of Marie Rogêt" and "Three Sundays in a Week." "The Mystery of Marie Rogêt," as Poe reveals in a succession of foot-notes, was built up on newspaper accounts of the murder of Mary Rogers at Weehawken, in June, 1841; [2] while "Three Sundays in a Week" is an ingenious reworking of a story, "Three Thurs-

---

[1] The *American Mercury*, xxiv, 218 (October, 1931).

[2] The plot of his companion story, "The Murders in the Rue Morgue," was also in every likelihood drawn from newspaper accounts, I may note in passing, though I have been unable to establish this. An apparent clue to its origin is an altogether circumstantial statement published anonymously in the Washington *Post* for October 3, 1912, according to which Poe's story originated in accounts of the murder of a Parisian courtesan, Rose Delacourt.

days in One Week," published in the Philadelphia *Public Ledger* for October 29, 1841.[1]

A very interesting example of Poe's use of materials found in contemporary magazines is afforded by his tale "The Pit and the Pendulum," which represents, as Professor D. L. Clark has shown,[2] the amalgamation of three stories from *Blackwood's*, — "The Man in the Bell," "The Iron Shroud," and "The Involuntary Experimentalist," — together with supplementary material from Charles Brockden Brown's *Edgar Huntley*. Other stories that seem to have been based, at least in part, on materials drawn from periodicals are "William Wilson," which appears to have had its origin in a similar story of double selfhood told by Irving in an article entitled "An Unwritten Drama of Lord Byron's" and published in the *Knickerbocker* for August, 1835;[3] "A Descent into the Maelström," which was probably suggested in part by the account of the Drontheim Whirlpool in *Alexander's Weekly Messenger* for October 10, 1838; and "The Premature Burial," which apparently drew its account of the burial alive of

[1] See the article of Miss F. N. Cherry in *American Literature*, ii, 232 f. (November, 1930).

[2] "The Sources of Poe's *The Pit and the Pendulum*," *Modern Language Notes*, xliv, 349 f. (June, 1929).

[3] vi, 142 f. — It was probably this article to which Irving referred in an entry in his Journal for July 18, 1859 (P. M. Irving's *Life of Irving*, iv, 305), in which he says that Poe wrote him on one occasion asking for permission to use material of his for a story; though possibly the reference was to materials used in his "Journal of Julius Rodman" (see below, p. 168). See also in this connection Woodberry, i, 232 n.

"Mademoiselle Victorine Lafourcade"[1] from the Philadelphia *Casket* of September, 1827.[2] It is possible, too, that the gory ending of "Berenice" was suggested by a paragraph in the Baltimore *Saturday Visiter* of February 23, 1833, about the robbing of graves "for the sake of obtaining *human teeth*," and that "Some Words with a Mummy" drew suggestions from a similar tale entitled "Letter from a Revived Mummy" published in the New York *Mirror* of January 21, 1832.[3] And it is altogether likely that his "X-ing a Paragrab" owes something to a skit entitled "Xtraordinary Play upon Xes," published in the *Mirror* for September 12, 1840.[4]

Still other stories grew out of Poe's interest in contemporary exploration. During the year preceding the publication of the first installment of his *Narrative of Arthur Gordon Pym* Poe had reviewed in the *Southern Literary Messenger* (August, 1836)[5] a report made to Congress by his friend J. N. Reynolds on a projected expedition into the South Seas, and from this report, as Mr. R. L. Rhea has shown,[6] he borrowed a good deal of the material that went into

[1] *Poe's Works*, v, 258 f. See also the suggestion of Miss Lucille King (University of Texas *Studies in English*, No. 10, pp. 128 f., 1930) to the effect that the incident of a "Mr. Stapleton" told by Poe in the same story (*Poe's Works*, v, 261 f.) is from a tale entitled "The Buried Alive" published in *Blackwood's* for October, 1821 (x, 262 f.).

[2] ii, 340 f.

[3] As Miss Lucille King has suggested in University of Texas *Studies in English*, No. 10, pp. 130 f. (1930).

[4] I am indebted for this suggestion to Mrs. Gladys E. Steen.

[5] *Poe's Works*, ix, 84 f.

[6] University of Texas *Studies in English*, No. 10, pp. 135 f. (1930).

his story, paraphrasing his original very closely at several points and actually reproducing without change in a few instances passages of a dozen words or more. For the same story Poe also borrowed freely from Captain Benjamin Morrell's *Narrative of Four Voyages, to the South Sea* (1832).[1]

Another of his stories in which he endeavors to capitalize the contemporary interest in exploration is "The Journal of Julius Rodman," which has to do, however, not with discoveries at sea, but with an expedition by land into the unexplored regions of the Northwest. For this story also he drew freely on the accounts of others. For much of his material, as Professor Woodberry has demonstrated,[2] he relied on Irving's *Astoria*; he also drew, as Mr. H. A. Turner has pointed out, on Irving's *The Adventures of Captain Bonneville*;[3] and he borrowed extensively from Lewis and Clark's *Expedition*,[4] in each instance resorting to the same method as that adopted in the composition of his *Arthur Gordon Pym*, — that of compilation and of close paraphrase.

And yet other stories are an outgrowth of Poe's interest in metaphysics and the natural sciences. "Bon-Bon" and "The Duc de L'Omelette" are farces in which would-be philosophers play the cen-

---

[1] *Poe's Works*, ed. Stedman and Woodberry, v, 355 f.; J. W. Robertson, *Poe: A Study*, San Francisco, 1921, p. 259.

[2] *Poe's Works*, ed. Stedman and Woodberry, v, 359 f.

[3] University of Texas *Studies in English*, No. 10, pp. 147 f.

[4] As Miss P. P. Crawford has shown: *ibid.*, No. 12, pp. 158 f. (1932).

tral rôles; "Morella" is made to turn upon the philosophical idea of identity, which Poe attributes to Schelling; [1] and "The Power of Words" is based on the ancient idea that "the source of all motion is thought." [2] Among stories that have to do with scientific problems are "A Descent into the Maelström," the climax of which is based on a principle which Poe attributes to Archimedes; [3] "Some Words with a Mummy," in which the galvanic battery is made to play an important part; and "The Strange Case of M. Valdemar" and "Mesmeric Revelation," both of which are concerned with the pseudo-science of mesmerism. [4] Semi-scientific also are his "Adventures of Hans Pfaall," which describes a balloon trip to the moon, and "The Balloon Hoax," in which Poe professes to give an account of the first crossing of the Atlantic in an air-ship.

In three of his sketches — "Landor's Cottage," "The Domain of Arnheim," and "The Landscape Garden" — he availed himself of the contemporary interest in landscape gardening. So, too, in "The Conversation of Eiros and Charmion" he capitalized the excitement aroused in the thirties and forties by Father Miller's predictions as to the end of the world,

[1] *Poe's Works*, II, 29.

[2] *Ibid.*, VI, 143.

[3] See *Modern Language Notes*, XLII, 520 (December, 1927).

[4] It has been suggested (see T. T. Watts, *Rambles and Reveries of an Art Student in Europe*, pp. 36 f.) that a partial source of this story was a novel, *The Seeress of Prevorst*, published by the Harpers, and advertised in the *Broadway Journal* of August 2, 1845 (II, 63).

— though he also avails himself, as Miss Alterton has shown, of a passage in Dr. Thomas Dick's *The Christian Philosopher*.[1] "The Oval Portrait" is said to have had its origin in a painting done by the artist Robert M. Sully.[2] And the original of Poe's description of the cottage in "Landor's Cottage" appears to have been, forsooth, a Currier and Ives print.[3]

Perhaps as many as a dozen of Poe's stories were suggested in some measure by the work of other novelists. "King Pest" was evidently founded on a chapter in Disraeli's *Vivian Grey*, in which we have an account of an adventure with a similar group of roisterers;[4] and "Metzengerstein" apparently borrowed Gothic details both from *Vivian Grey* and from *The Castle of Otranto*.[5] "Lionizing" is an extravaganza done in the manner of Bulwer's "Too Handsome for Anything."[6] "Silence. A Fable" appears to have drawn hints from Bulwer's "Monos and Daimonos";[7] and "The Cask of Amontillado" has perhaps profited by a scene in *The Last Days of Pompeii*.[8] The incident of the walling up of the victim in "The Cask of Amontillado" probably goes back to a similar incident in Balzac's story "La

[1] *Origins of Poe's Critical Theory*, p. 141.
[2] See Miss Phillips, *Poe — the Man*, p. 691.
[3] As suggested by Professor Henry S. Canby in his *Classic Americans*, New York [1931], p. 273.
[4] *Poe's Works*, ed. Stedman and Woodberry, IV, 295.
[5] University of Texas *Studies in English*, No. 10, p. 129 (1930).
[6] Woodberry, I, 130.
[7] *Poe's Works*, ed. Stedman and Woodberry, IV, 296.
[8] Bk. IV, chap. 13.

Grande Bretèche." [1] "The Mask of the Red Death" is pretty clearly indebted to William Harrison Ainsworth's *Old Saint Paul's*.[2] "A Tale of Jerusalem" borrowed its title from the sub-title adopted by Horace Smith for his novel *Zillah* (1828), and also much of its detail, with here and there a phrase from the same source.[3]

Professor Palmer Cobb [4] has endeavored to show that several of Poe's plots were borrowed from the tales of E. T. A. Hoffmann. And he has proved his case, in my judgment, in at least one instance,— that of Poe's early story "The Assignation," which he derives from Hoffmann's "Doge und Dogaressa," [5] a story that has the same setting, essentially the same major characters, and a closely parallel situation involving a liaison between the heroine, who has married (against the will of the doge of Venice) a young man to whom she is indebted for the rescue from drowning of her child (as with Poe) or of her husband (as with Hoffmann).

[1] H. S. Canby and others, in their *English Composition*, New York, 1909, pp. 348 f., have reprinted these two stories side by side.

[2] *Transactions of the American Philological Association* for 1907, p. xxxi. It is possible, I think, that Poe also owed something to an account by N. P. Willis in the New York *Mirror* for June 2, 1832 (IX, 380), of a masked ball that he had attended in Paris, in the course of which there was a "cholera waltz" and a "cholera galopade," and a masked figure impersonating the "Cholera itself."

[3] James Southall Wilson, in the *American Mercury*, XXIV, 215 f. (October, 1931).

[4] *The Influence of E. T. A. Hoffman on the Tales of Edgar Allan Poe* Chapel Hill, North Carolina, 1908.

[5] *Ibid.*, pp. 81 f.

An extremely interesting example of the transformation which Poe was capable of bringing about in a story borrowed from another is afforded by his gruesome tale "Hop-Frog," which was obviously based on an incident from Froissart's *Chronicles*, an account of a mumming held at the court of Charles VI in celebration of a state marriage. This story as Poe found it (in the *Broadway Journal* of February 1, 1845,[1] while he was one of its editors) was merely a bald recounting of the historical incident with little or nothing of the dramatic; but Poe has made out of it a vividly tragic story of revenge, introducing also a "touch of fantasy" in representing the king and his squires as appearing in the guise of ourang-outangs.

"The Gold-Bug" is unique among Poe's stories in that it is built up on an American legend, that of Captain Kidd's buried treasure. Irving had treated the same legend in "The Devil and Tom Walker," as had also Poe's friend R. M. Bird in his *Sheppard Lee* (1836). With both of these narratives Poe was doubtless familiar, and it may well be that he derived hints for his story from *Sheppard Lee*,[2] in which we have not only the digging for gold under a huge tree in a forest, but two characters that correspond roughly to Legrand and Jupiter, the chief characters in "The Gold-Bug."[3] But Poe probably relied much

[1] I, 71.
[2] Poe had reviewed *Sheppard Lee* in the *Southern Literary Messenger* for September, 1836 (*Poe's Works*, IX, 126 f.).
[3] See the *Nation*, XC, 625 f. (June 23, 1910).

less on his reading in this instance than was usual with him, evidently utilizing for the first half of the story reminiscences of his stay at Charleston while in the army, and capitalizing very ingeniously for the second half of the story his knowledge of cryptography.

Another illustration of Poe's resourcefulness in utilizing materials near at hand is afforded by "The Thousand-and-Second Tale of Scheherazade," which owes its framework to the *Arabian Nights*, but is largely a catalogue of the marvels of modern invention, as the steamboat, the railway train, the daguerreotype, the incubator, and the like.[1] Three other stories, "The Spectacles," "The Man that was Used Up," and "Why the Little Frenchman Wears his Hand in a Sling," were apparently drawn from even less remote sources, being little more than elaborations of anecdotes which Poe had probably heard in conversation.

For several of his stories Poe made use of materials that he found in encyclopædias. For "A Descent into the Maelström" he borrowed important details from an early edition of the *Encyclopædia Britannica*;[2] in "Some Words with a Mummy" he paraphrased passages from two articles in the *Encyclopedia Americana*;[3] and for "The Adventures of

[1] The same basic plot, it may be noted, Washington Irving had adopted some twenty years before for his farce *Abou Hassan*, using as his immediate source Von Weber's opera of the same name.

[2] *Poe's Works*, ed. Stedman and Woodberry, IV, 290 f.

[3] See University of Texas *Studies in English*, No. 10, pp. 131 f. (1930). It is possible also to account for the names of a number of Poe's

Hans Pfaall" he borrowed in like fashion from *Rees's Cyclopædia*.¹ Other instances of a similar appropriation of materials are afforded by "A Tale of the Ragged Mountains," in which he copied with immaterial changes a passage from Macaulay's "Warren Hastings," ² and "The Balloon Hoax," for which, as Professor W. B. Norris has shown,³ he paraphrased at length from several contemporary accounts of ballooning.⁴

Besides these more tangible indebtednesses there were also literary indebtednesses of a less palpable nature. The influence of Defoe is, I think, reflected, in *Arthur Gordon Pym* and other early stories, in the

characters. "William Wilson" was the name of one of John Allan's agents in England, a Quaker who lived first in Cheapside and later at Kendal. "Wormley" and "Thornton," from the "Journal of Julius Rodman," and "Preston" from "William Wilson," are names of Virginia families with which Poe was familiar. "Julius Rodman" is, I suspect, a modification of the given names of Joseph Rodman Drake. The name "Dupin" was in all likelihood suggested by the family name of "George Sand," Madame Dupin. "Pauline Dubourg" in "The Murders in the Rue Morgue" must have been suggested by the proprietors of the school which Poe attended in London in 1816–1817. It is not mere coincidence, I suspect, that characters bearing the surnames "Alexandre" and "Dumas" appear in close juxtaposition in the same story. Poe had employed a similar makeshift in his *Politian* in utilizing the given name of Baldassare Castiglione for one of his characters and the surname for another.

¹ See the article of Mr. M. N. Posey in *Modern Language Notes*, XLV, 505 f. (December, 1930).

² Cf. Henry Austin in *Literature* for August 4, 1899.

³ See the *Nation*, XCI, 389 f. (October 27, 1910).

⁴ Certain of Poe's titles, moreover, were evidently drawn from his reading. "Eiros and Charmion" must have come from Shakespeare's *Antony and Cleopatra*. "Monos and Una" (involving one of Poe's many puns) was perhaps suggested by Bulwer's title "Monos and Daimonos." "Diddling Considered as One of the Exact Sciences" involves a reminis-

simplicity and downrightness of style, and in the ingenious methods employed in the interest of verisimilitude.[1] The influence of Sterne is evident in "Lionizing." I have fancied that Dickens's example helps to account for "The Man of the Crowd," and that the influence of De Quincey asserts itself in the ornateness and the mellowness of style in "The Masque of the Red Death."[2] Hawthorne seems for once to have influenced Poe in "The Oval Portrait";[3] and the influence of Irving's humor is unmistakable in "Hans Pfaall" and "The Devil in the Belfry."

In a good many of his stories Poe dealt afresh with materials that he had used in earlier stories. "Morella," for instance, was, as Poe admitted in a letter to Philip Pendleton Cooke,[4] a fore-study for "Ligeia"; "The Duc de L'Omelette" appears to have been a fore-study for "Bon-Bon";[5] and "A Predicament" treats a situation that was later to appear in "The Devil in the Belfry" and "The Pit and the Pendulum." In like manner the plot of

cence of James Kenney's *Jeremy Diddler*. "A Tale of Jerusalem" adopts as its title the sub-title of Horace Smith's *Zillah*. "Mellonta Tauta" is from the *Antigone* of Sophocles, the rejected titles "Siope" and "Epimanes" are adaptations of common nouns from the Greek, and "Ligeia," "Berenice," and "The Sphinx" obviously go back to Greek myth.

[1] There are also passages in *Arthur Gordon Pym* and "MS. Found in a Bottle" that suggest the influence of "The Rime of the Ancient Mariner."

[2] A parallel in situation between De Quincey's *Klosterheim* and Poe's "The Masque of the Red Death" may also be worth noting.

[3] As well in substance as in style.   [4] *Poe's Works*, XVII, 52 ff.

[5] Or did "Bon-Bon" serve as a fore-study for "The Duc de L'Omelette," in spite of the fact that "The Duc de L'Omelette" was published ahead of it?

"The Tell-Tale Heart" furnished also the plot of "The Black Cat," and much the same situation as underlies "The Business Man" reappears in "Diddling Considered as One of the Exact Sciences."[1]

For some of the tales, there is, in my judgment, little occasion to look for a source outside of Poe's own fancy. Possessed of an acute and inquiring mind, Poe took pleasure in wrestling with problems of science and of philosophy, and especially in the analysis of situation. Thus it seems not improbable that "The Man of the Crowd" had its origin merely in the attempt on the part of the poet to analyze the situation presented by the initial incident of the story, that of a character obsessed by the idea of not being alone. So, also, "The Tell-Tale Heart" and "The Colloquy of Monos and Una" may be merely the elaboration of situations which the poet had conceived independently of anything he had read; and it is possible, I think, that "The Fall of the House of Usher" had a similar genesis.

---

[1] Here also may be mentioned the interplay between Poe's tales and poems. The death of a beautiful woman, or, more precisely, the grief occasioned by her death, which furnished the theme of "The Raven" and still other poems, is also dealt with in "Ligeia" and "Morella" and "Berenice." The realm of departed spirits, which Poe treats in half a dozen of his poems, is also the theme of "Silence. A Fable." There is interplay, too, between Poe's stories and his expository prose. "Mesmeric Revelation," for instance, contains passages that anticipate passages in *Eureka*; "The Business Man" has something in common with the essay entitled "Peter Snook"; and the second half of "The Gold-Bug" is related to the papers on cryptography.

A good many of Poe's stories, moreover, as I have already shown, are in some sense autobiographical: see above, pp. 135 f.

With regard to Poe's methods of working with his borrowed materials, there is, I think, nothing new or unfamiliar to those acquainted with the methods employed by others. In his article "Peter Snook" Poe declares that "to originate is carefully, patiently, and understandingly to combine." [1] The process of composition with him was very largely that of combination, the combining of borrowed materials with materials evolved from his own experience and thinking, but always with more or less of modification, and a pretty constant effort to concentrate and focus and vivify.

Certain formulas as to his practice will help to explain his methods. A score or more of his tales represent the elaboration of some borrowed incident or situation, with which is combined material evoked out of his own brain or from his own experience. This is the case with his "William Wilson," for instance, or with "The Premature Burial." A few of the tales, as "The Pit and the Pendulum," involve the combination of several borrowed stories or situations. Still others, as "The Business Man" and "The Thousand-and-Second Tale of Scheherazade," are the product of a combination of miscellaneous materials, largely expository or descriptive in nature, which are incorporated in a narrative framework. And yet others, as "Shadow. A Parable" or "The Man of the Crowd," involve the analysis and elaboration of some situation or mood; while others, — a

[1] *Poe's Works*, xiv, 73.

good many others, — as "The Pit and the Pendulum," "The Power of Words," "A Descent into the Maelström," "The Imp of the Perverse," and "The Colloquy of Monos and Una," represent the development of some idea (philosophical, psychological, scientific, or pseudo-scientific). These five formulas will, I believe, account for the evolution of four-fifths of Poe's stories.[1]

IV

I come finally to a consideration of Poe's critical and miscellaneous essays.

I have said that Poe turned to the writing of stories as a means of making a living. If this was true of his stories, how much more true it was of his critical and editorial writing, most of it hack work, to which he was driven by stern necessity. That he acquired

---

[1] How far Poe is to be held blamable for his borrowings from others for his stories is a matter upon which opinion has differed. Dr. John W. Robertson holds (*Poe: A Study*, p. 259) that he has in no way exceeded his rights in his extensive paraphrasing of passages from Morrell's *Voyages* in his *Arthur Gordon Pym*. On the other hand, Professor W. D. Armes would have it (*Transactions of the American Philological Association* for 1907, p. xxxi) that in borrowing from Disraeli's *Vivian Grey* suggestions for the account of the debauch that furnishes the central situation in "King Pest" — an account for which he carried over no word of Disraeli's — he has committed a serious offense. For my own part, I cannot feel that Poe in such debt as he incurred to Disraeli in this instance has violated the proprieties, for he has freely recast his borrowed material, has, I think, improved upon his original, and has set unmistakably the mark of his own individuality upon the story. But I find it difficult to acquit Poe of all guilt in his copying from Morrell for his *Pym*, and so also with his appropriations from Irving in "Julius Rodman" and from Macaulay in "A Tale of the Ragged Mountains."

extraordinary deftness in handling the book-review, and that he at times found genuine pleasure in his work as editor and reviewer, scarcely affects the truth of this observation.

His first reviewing was probably done in Baltimore after his return from West Point in 1831, though just how soon thereafter we do not know. It is not improbable that he was employed on some Philadelphia newspaper,[1] forwarding his articles from Baltimore, as he was presently to forward his reviews to Richmond for the *Messenger*. At all events, he had become known to the editors of the Baltimore newspapers by 1835, and had little difficulty in procuring publication there of brief notices of successive issues of the *Messenger*.[2] And that he had become interested in criticism even before going to Baltimore is proved by his "Letter to B——," first published as the "Preface" of his *Poems* of 1831.

What served him as models for his reviews is a matter of interesting speculation. In every likelihood he found his models largely in the British magazines of the day, which also furnished him aid of various sorts, as we have seen, in fabricating the materials for his stories. There was, to be sure, something in the Southern temper of a hundred years ago that helps to explain him. Was it unnatural that frankness and independence and open-mindedness

---

[1] As Mr. J. H. Whitty holds (*The Poems of Poe*, p. xxxvi), on the authority of Poe's friend, F. W. Thomas.

[2] See the notice in the Baltimore *Republican* for May 14, 1835, and see also Woodberry, I, 113 f.

should characterize the work of one who grew up almost under the shadow of Monticello? The sharpness of some of his criticisms, too, may be explained in a measure by the fieriness of mood well known in the lower South and not unknown in Virginia, — as exhibited by John Randolph of Roanoke, for instance, or by Beverly Tucker, whom the lamented Mr. Parrington has placed along with the "fire-eaters." [1]

But I am convinced that the chief explanation of his occasional severity and his habitual outspokenness, not to mention other commendable traits, in his reviewing, is to be found in the example set by the British reviewers, and that he was largely indebted to the British reviewers of his generation and the generation immediately preceding him, — to Jeffrey and Kit North and Gifford and Hazlitt and Macaulay. Though he satirized *Blackwood's* in several instances, he nevertheless followed the example of its crusty editor by showing neither fear nor favor in his own critical judgments. He early established a familiarity with the current British magazines,[2] and he evidently had access also, particularly during his Baltimore period,[3] to back numbers of the magazines.[4]

[1] V. L. Parrington, *Main Currents in American Thought*, New York, 1927, ii, 36.

[2] Indirectly, also, he may have been influenced by the example of American magazines and weeklies in their all but habitual indulgence in laudation of their own authors and their own things, a practice that Poe abhorred and that he let slip no opportunity to condemn.

[3] At which time he did some of his most fruitful reading.

[4] According to Mr. Hervey Allen (*Israfel*, p. 129) the firm of Ellis and Allan imported the current British magazines, and sold them over their counters.

Both Wilson and Hazlitt he reviewed once or oftener; and he also noticed on various occasions Macaulay's critical essays, praising them without stint at almost every point.[1]

Macaulay's example probably meant a good deal to him by way of suggesting to him the value of concreteness and of analysis; and it has been suggested, not without plausibility, that Macaulay's smashing review of Montgomery's poems helped to confirm in him the disposition to "use up" an occasional victim.[2]

He owed something, too, I suspect, to Hazlitt, whose boldness and plain speaking naturally aroused his admiration; and it is not unlikely that he derived from Hazlitt the suggestion of his doctrine of "indefinitiveness" as one of the cardinal virtues of the lyric, a theory that Hazlitt had put forward in his essay "On Poetry in General" in 1818.

But his greatest indebtedness as critic was, beyond any doubt, to Coleridge. In particular, he was indebted to the *Biographia Literaria* for the suggestion of his earliest definition of poetry as embodied in his "Letter to B——," which takes as a point of departure Coleridge's famous differentiation between poetry and science. He was also influenced by Coleridge's well-known differentiation between imagination and fancy, to which he adverts more than once in his reviews; and he perhaps owed to him also,

[1] *Poe's Works*, x, 156 f.; xiii, 193 f.; xiv, 191.
[2] F. C. Prescott, *Poe's Critical Essays*, New York, 1909, pp. xxxiv f.

as Prescott [1] suggests, the idea that a long poem cannot exist. At least indirectly he must also have been obligated to Wordsworth, whose critical prefaces he had read,[2] and whose insistence upon instruction as an end in art doubtless helped him to clarify his own thinking on the subject and thus opened the way to his vigorous repudiation of didacticism.

He perhaps owed something also to August Wilhelm Schlegel, with whom he associates, in an early review in the *Southern Literary Messenger*,[3] the doctrine of "unity or totality of interest," out of which he presently developed the idea which lies at the base of his famous definition of the short story, that of "unity or totality of effect." [4]

Of more specific sources it may be noted that in the case of his review of Stephens's *Arabia Petræa*, a critique on which he plumed himself, he made use of materials supplied him by the classical scholar Dr. Charles Anthon.[5] And he probably did a good deal more of the same sort of thing.

In other instances, as we know, — and I suspect in a good many other instances, — he adopted the short cut of paraphrasing or copying outright from the

---

[1] *Poe's Critical Essays*, p. xxxiii. See also the article of Professor Floyd Stovall, "Poe's Debt to Coleridge," in the University of Texas *Studies in English*, No. 10, pp. 93 f. (1930).

[2] Prescott, p. xxxii.

[3] II, 113 (January, 1836); *Poe's Works*, VIII, 126. See also Prescott, pp. xxx f., and Stovall, p. 93.

[4] In his review of Hawthorne's *Twice-Told Tales* in *Graham's Magazine*, *Poe's Works*, XI, 104 f.

[5] *Ibid.*, X, 1 f.; XVII, 42 f.

book under review,— much as he did in his borrowings for a number of his stories. This was done extensively in his review of Irving's *Astoria*,[1] for which he carried over, with immaterial changes, a dozen or more pages from Irving's book.

As for his miscellaneous prose writings, Professor Woodberry has shown that he levied on Brewster's *Letters on Natural Magic* for some of the information embodied in his article on "Maelzel's Chess-Player";[2] and it is plain that he drew upon Newton, Laplace, Kepler, Humboldt, Sir John Herschel, Leverrier, and others for the materials underlying his *Eureka*. Miss Alterton has recently shown that he borrowed at one point in *Eureka* from Dr. Dick's *The Christian Philosopher*, a semi-popular treatise of the day;[3] and Mr. M. N. Posey has drawn attention to the fact that he also embodied a passage from *Rees's Cyclopædia* in his notes on *Eureka*.[4]

For his "Literary Small Talk," as Mr. T. O. Mabbott has pointed out, he borrowed from Gibbon's *Decline and Fall of the Roman Empire*.[5] For his "Pinakidia" he ransacked such works as Disraeli's *Curiosities of Literature*, Montgomery's *Lectures on Literature*, Bryant's *Mythology*, and Bielfeld's *Les Premiers Traits de l'Érudition Universelle*.[6] At least

[1] *Ibid.*, ix, 207 f.
[2] Woodberry, i, 178.
[3] *Origins of Poe's Critical Theory*, pp. 138 f.
[4] *Modern Language Notes*, xlv, 507 (December, 1930).
[5] *Doings of Gotham*, p. 27.
[6] *American Literature*, i, 197 f. (May, 1929).

one of his "Marginalia," the pun on the quail, he borrowed from Sheridan.[1]

And there is the unhappy story of the composition of his *Conchologist's First Book*. For this work, which reveals Poe's creative powers at their lowest ebb, and which furnishes one of the unhappiest chapters in his history, he paraphrased or boldly copied virtually everything in the volume from a similar treatise by a Captain Thomas Brown. It scarcely affects the case that Poe withdrew his name from the title-page of the book when attention was publicly called to his appropriation of another's materials, — though it must be conceded that the circumstances attending his connection with the volume, in which he collaborated with a Dr. Wyatt, are not entirely clear.[2] But the case seems bad enough, whatever may be the extenuating circumstances. Poe's defense of himself when publicly pilloried for what he appears to have done was that "*all* school-books are necessarily made in a similar way." [3]

[1] See Brander Matthews, *Pen and Ink*, p. 37. As Professor Carl Schreiber has shown (the *Colophon*, II, 2 [May, 1930]), he borrowed another from Prince Pückler-Moskau, *The Tour of a Prince* (as translated by Sarah Austin).

[2] See *Poe's Works*, I, 146 f.; Woodberry, I, 194 f.; Allen, *Israfel*, pp. 442 f., 627; Miss Mary E. Phillips, *Poe — the Man*, pp. 562 f.; and Gardner Teall, the New York *Times*, December 3, 1922. Mr. Teall, it may be noted, minimizes Poe's guilt in the matter.

[3] *Poe's Works*, XVII, 278; the University of Virginia *Alumni Bulletin*, XVII, 46 (January, 1924).

V

I began my discussion of Poe's origins with the statement that much has already been done by way of
revealing the poet's sources. I shall conclude with
the statement that much yet remains to be done. In
particular, I think we may look forward to having
fuller information as to the origins of Poe's stories.
A good deal will come out, if I am not much mistaken,
with a more thorough examination of the newspapers
and magazines of Poe's time; and I look for further
revelations to follow upon a closer examination of
French and German literature. Are there perhaps
prototypes of his early farces, "Bon-Bon" and "The
Duc de L'Omelette," in French literature? Did he
owe anything to Voltaire? With the passing of time
more light will also be thrown, I believe, on the origins of his critical theory. What, if anything, did he
owe to Schlegel? Was he influenced by Novalis? [1]
And how much and what did he owe to the German
philosophers?

I shall venture one further generalization as to
Poe's method of working with his sources. It has
frequently been said that his method as artist was
thoroughly mechanical: this is what Mr. Lewis Mumford meant,[2] if I read him aright, when he asserted
that Poe's world was "plutonian like that of Watt

[1] See the suggestion of Paul Elmer More, *Studies in Philology*, xx,
304 (July, 1923).
[2] *The Golden Day*, New York, 1926, p. 76.

and Fulton and Gradgrind." I am aware that Poe's account of the composition of "The Raven" lends color to such a view; and so also with the too obviously mechanical nature of some of his poems — as "Lenore" in its final form — and of some of his stories, — as "William Wilson" and "The Business Man"; and so also with what we know of his habits of revision. But I am not sure that this theory will hold for the bulk of Poe's work. On the contrary, I wonder whether Poe's methods of composition in the case of most of his poems and tales were radically different from the methods employed by other artists of whatever age or race.

THE POE CANON[1]

I

THE first collective edition of Poe's works was that of Rufus W. Griswold, published in four volumes, the first three volumes in 1850 and the fourth in 1856.[2] The latest collective edition is that of Professor James A. Harrison, comprising sixteen volumes and published in 1902.[3] The Griswold edition contains 42 poems, 68 tales, and 74 essays and miscellaneous prose articles. The Harrison edition — otherwise known as the "Virginia Poe" — contains 55 poems (including seven "poems attributed to Poe"), 70 tales, and no less than 285 essays and miscellaneous articles. There are listed, also, in the edition, in a bibliography printed in the appendix of the sixteenth volume,[4] some forty other items which are not reprinted in that edition. There are a good many items that have been ascribed to Poe at one time or

[1] Reprinted, with revisions and additions, from the *Publications of the Modern Language Association of America*, xxvii, 325 f. (September, 1912).

[2] *The Works of the Late Edgar Allan Poe*, ed. R. W. Griswold, 4 vols., New York, 1850, 1856.

[3] *The Complete Works of Edgar Allan Poe*, ed. J. A. Harrison, 17 vols., New York [1902]. Referred to in this volume as *Poe's Works*.

[4] *Ibid.*, xvi, 355 f.

another that are not included in Harrison's bibliography. Among these are some twenty-five poems, six tales, and upwards of fifty brief essays, making in all more than four score poems, 77 tales, and over four hundred essays of one sort or another that have been attributed to Poe.

The growth of the Poe canon is thus seen to have been extraordinary. The increase is to be traced to several circumstances. In the first place, Griswold, although he professed to publish everything that Poe would have wished to preserve,[1] omitted a number of things that must surely have been known to him, and others, probably, through oversight.[2] There must have been a good many things, too, that were inaccessible to him, and some things, no doubt, of which he was entirely ignorant. It is reasonably clear that Poe had not preserved any very full collection of his writings. He wrote Lowell, for instance, in 1844 that he had not saved copies of any of the volumes of his poems, and that at that time he had "on hand" only one of his stories, "The Gold-Bug." [3] So far as we know, moreover, he had not taken the trouble to make up any very exhaustive list of his publications. And most of his essays — especially his editorial and critical essays — had been published anonymously, while some of them had appeared in extremely out-of-the-way places.

[1] *Poe's Works*, ed. Griswold, iv, v.

[2] He omitted, among other things, the early lines "To Helen," beginning, "Helen, thy beauty is to me," and the tale entitled "The Elk."

[3] Woodberry, ii, 94 f.

Small wonder, then, if Griswold missed a good many things.

The main discoveries of new items have been made by Mr. J. H. Ingram, Professor George E. Woodberry, Professor James A. Harrison, Mr. J. H. Whitty, and Professor Thomas Ollive Mabbott. To Mr. Ingram it fell a good many years ago to establish Poe's authorship of "The Journal of Julius Rodman,"[1] a tale of more than 25,000 words published anonymously in *Burton's Gentleman's Magazine* in 1840, when Poe was one of its editors. Professor Woodberry succeeded not long afterwards in turning up, in a New York annual, Poe's tale "The Elk" (or "Morning on the Wissahiccon");[2] and he subsequently brought to light a fragment of another tale, "The Light-house."[3] Professor Harrison was the first to present at all adequately Poe's contributions to the *Southern Literary Messenger* and the *Broadway Journal*, printing in his edition more than a hundred brief articles that had been either overlooked or ignored by former editors. Mr. J. H. Whitty has called attention to a half-dozen or more new poems that he attributes to Poe, and he has in addition drawn attention to some neglected prose items in

[1] Through the discovery of a letter in which Poe acknowledges the authorship of this story (Ingram, p. 145).

[2] Of which mention had been made in the list of Poe's tales enumerated by Lowell, in his sketch of Poe in *Graham's* for February, 1845.

[3] This he found in manuscript among the Griswold Papers. It is published in Woodberry's revised life of Poe, Boston, 1909, II, 397 f.

Burton's Gentleman's Magazine.[1] Other uncollected items have been pointed out by B. B. Minor (several short papers in the *Southern Literary Messenger*),[2] by Professor John C. French (a signed poem and two other poems perhaps by Poe, in the Baltimore *Saturday Visiter* for 1833),[3] by Professor Thomas Ollive Mabbott (several articles contributed to Thomas Dunn English's *Aristidean* and articles in the *Democratic Review*, the Pittsburgh *Literary Examiner*,[4] and the Philadelphia *Public Ledger*), by Miss Margaret Alterton (sundry articles in the *Southern Literary Messenger* and *Burton's Gentleman's Magazine*),[5] by Miss Mary E. Phillips (a dozen or more items, including articles in *Blackwood's Magazine*),[6] and by myself (some forty miscellaneous articles, mainly reviews and editorials, in the *Southern Literary Messenger*, *Burton's Gentleman's Magazine*, *Graham's Magazine*, the *Broadway Journal*, and the New York *Evening Mirror*).[7]

In the course of these many accretions, it is but natural that some things should have crept into the

[1] *The Complete Poems of Edgar Allan Poe*, Boston, 1911, pp. 139 f., and *passim*.

[2] See his volume, *The Southern Literary Messenger, 1834–1864*, New York, 1905, pp. 37, 42, 45.

[3] *Modern Language Notes*, XXXIII, 259 f. (May, 1918).

[4] The *American Mercury*, II, 205 (June, 1924); *Doings of Gotham*, ed. J. E. Spannuth and T. O. Mabbott, pp. 23 f.

[5] *Origins of Poe's Critical Theory*, Iowa City, 1925, *passim*.

[6] *Poe — the Man*, pp. 712 f. and *passim*.

[7] The New York *Nation*, LXXXIX, 623 f., 647 f. (December 23 and 30, 1909); *ibid.*, XC, 62 (January 20, 1910); *Modern Language Notes*, XXXII, 267 f. (May, 1917).

canon which on closer examination must be rejected from it, and that certain other things should have been admitted that are of doubtful authenticity. It stands to reason, too, that some things belonging to Poe should have eluded the search of his editors and bibliographers. The purpose of this paper is to inquire into the genuineness of a number of items that appear to be either spurious or of doubtful authority, and to indicate where further additions to the canon may possibly be found.

II

(A) *Poems.* — Of poems that have been erroneously ascribed to Poe there are upwards of a score. First of all, there are ten or a dozen pieces that have at some time been ascribed to the poet but that have subsequently been shown to be the work of other hands. These include "My Soul," a brief poem written by a student of the University of Virginia and published as a "Poe find" in one of the University annuals; [1] Hood's sonnet on "Silence," which Poe published in *Burton's Gentleman's Magazine* above his own initial, and which I, misled by this, once attempted to saddle upon him; [2] "Kelah," a piece of doggerel (sometimes entitled "The Murderer") which is from time to time resurrected and

[1] Reproduced in facsimile in the Richmond *Dispatch* for January 17, 1909.

[2] See the New York *Nation*, December 30, 1909, and January 20, 1910.

proclaimed to the world as a Poe discovery; some crude lines beginning "O, where shall our waking be," published above Poe's initials in the New York *Tribune* of August 27, 1845, and later assigned to a writer using the initials "E. A. S." (E. A. Stansbury?);[1] four short poems—"To Isadore," "The Village Street," "The Forest Reverie," and "Annette" — from the pen of A. M. Ide, published in the *Broadway Journal* in 1845, and tentatively attributed to Poe by Mr. John H. Ingram;[2] a parody of "The Raven" by Harriet Winslow, published originally in *Graham's Magazine* in April, 1848;[3] a part of one of Mrs. Osgood's earlier poems, "Woman's Trust, a Dramatic Sketch," impliedly given to Poe by John Pendleton Kennedy in his *Autograph Leaves of American Authors* (in which an excerpt from the poem appears in facsimile in Poe's autograph);[4] a part of S. Anna Lewis's poem "The Forsaken";[5] "Lilitha," an imitation of "Ulalume," now known to be the work of F. G. Fairfield;[6] and "Leonainie," assigned to Poe by a contributor to the

---

[1] The *Broadway Journal*, August 30, 1845.

[2] Ingram, *The Complete Poetical Works of Edgar Allen* (*sic*) *Poe*, New York [1888], pp. 178 f. Cf. also *Poe's Works*, vii, pp. 226, 228 f., and James L. Onderdonk, *History of American Verse*, Chicago, 1901, p. 243.

[3] A facsimile of the poem as copied by Poe appears in the New York *Journal* for March 15, 1896. See the New York *Times* for November 27 and December 11, 1909.

[4] *Autograph Leaves of American Authors*, ed. J. P. Kennedy and Alexander Bliss, Baltimore, 1864.

[5] The New York *Times* for December 4 and December 11, 1909.

[6] The *Southern Bivouac*, v, 298 (October, 1886).

Fortnightly Review in 1904,[1] but later shown to have been written by James Whitcomb Riley.[2]

There are also several poems still attributed to Poe by one or more of his editors or biographers which we can be sure are not his work. These are: (1) a translation of the Greek "Hymn in Honor of Harmodius and Aristogiton," first published in the *Southern Literary Messenger* for December, 1835;[3] (2) "The Mammoth Squash," which appeared in Thomas Dunn English's *Aristidean*, October, 1845;[4] (3) "The Poets and Poetry of America," a satire in verse published under the pseudonym "Lavante" at Philadelphia in 1847;[5] (4) "The Fire-Fiend," which first appeared in the New York *Saturday Press*, November 19, 1859.[6]

(1) It may be argued in favor of Poe's authorship of the "Hymn in Honor of Harmodius and Aristogiton" — first attributed to Poe by Ingram,[7] and also included by Harrison and Whitty in their editions of the poems (under "Poems Attributed to Poe" in each instance)[8] — that the article containing the translation is subscribed with Poe's initial and that Poe, who was the editor of the *Messenger* when the poem appeared, had signed at least one article known

---

[1] The *Fortnightly Review*, LXXXI, 329 f. (February, 1904). See also in this connection a strange pamphlet, *Edgar Allan Poe*, by Alfred Russell Wallace, New York [1930].

[2] The *Fortnightly Review*, LXXXI, 706 f.   [3] II, 38.

[4] Republished by Harrison in *Poe's Works*, VII, 236.

[5] *Ibid.*, pp. 246 f.; VII, 246 f.

[6] *Ibid.*, pp. 239 f.   [7] *Life and Letters of Poe*, pp. 52 f.

[8] *Poe's Works*, VII, 250; Whitty, p. 158.

to be his in the same way.[1] But there is an article in the *Messenger* for March, 1848,[2] in which the writer, who signs himself "M.," expressly claims the authorship of the translation for himself. Examination of the files of the *Messenger* reveals that "M." was one of the signatures used by Lucian Minor, a gifted lawyer of Louisa County, Virginia, and at one time Professor of Law at William and Mary College. Minor had contributed to the *Messenger* from its beginning. Poe, in subscribing his initial to the article containing the poem, did not mean, I take it, to set up any claim to its authorship.

(2) "The Mammoth Squash" is included among the "Poems Attributed to Poe" by both Harrison [3] and Whitty.[4] But it is clear enough from the context in which the lines originally appeared that they were not by Poe, but were intended as a hoax, as was the case, also, with the verses accompanying them and attributed to Longfellow, Whittier, and others.[5]

(3) The "Lavante" booklet, which adopts the title of Griswold's famous anthology, *The Poets and Poetry of America*, was first attributed to Poe by Mr. Oliver Leigh, writing under the pen-name "Geoffrey Quarles," in a pamphlet on the subject [6]

---

[1] See the article entitled "Palestine" in the *Messenger* for February, 1836 (II, 152).

[2] XIV, 185.   [3] VII, 236.

[4] *Poe's Poems*, pp. 159 f.

[5] *Poe's Works*, VII, 236. A similar hoax at Poe's expense appeared in *Godey's Lady's Book* for December, 1849 (XXXIX, 419), together with a facsimile of Poe's autograph.

[6] *The Poets and Poetry of America*, New York, 1887.

in which a reprint of the satire is included. Leigh holds that the poem is nothing other than Poe's "American Parnassus" (or "The Authors of America in Prose and Verse," as Poe sometimes styled it), a critical treatise on the celebrities of Poe's time, on which we know, from various allusions to it in his letters, he was engaged during several years after his return to New York in 1844. That this view is erroneous is evident, I think, from the style of the poem. But there is conclusive demonstration that the article is not Poe's in a letter of his, of the date December 15, 1846,[1] in which the projected volume is described in some detail. Alluding to his "Literati" articles in *Godey's* (1846), Poe says: "The unexpected circulation of the series, also, suggested to me that I might make a hit and some profit . . . by extending the plan into that of *a book* on American Letters generally, and keeping the publication in my own hands." Continuing, he writes: "I am now *at* this — body and soul. I intend to be thorough . . . to examine analytically . . . all the salient points of Literature in general — *e. g.*, Poetry, The Drama, Criticism, Historical Writing, Versification, &c., &c. You may get an idea of the manner in which I propose to write the whole book, by reading the notice of Hawthorne which will appear in the January 'Godey,'[2] as well as the article on 'The Rationale

[1] *Poe's Works*, XVII, 269 f.; J. S. Wilson, University of Virginia *Alumni Bulletin*, XVII, 40 f. (January, 1924).

[2] It did not appear till November. It is reprinted in *Poe's Works*, XIII, 141 f.

of Verse.'" This makes it plain that the "Parnassus" was in prose and that it dealt with prose writers as well as with writers of verse; the "Lavante" pamphlet is in verse, and deals only with "poets and poetry." Mr. Whitty is, I think, right in his conjecture [1] that Poe's "Parnassus" was the same as his "Living Writers of America," certain notes for the prospectus of which are still in existence.

(4) Both Stedman and Gill believed "The Fire-Fiend" to be Poe's, and Professor Harrison also inclined to the same view.[2] But C. D. Gardette, who first attributed the poem to Poe (in the New York *Saturday Press* of November 19, 1859), subsequently published a pamphlet — *The Whole Truth in the Question of the Fire-Fiend*, Philadelphia, 1864 — in which he admits that he composed the piece himself.[3]

Besides these there are several other poems that have been attributed to Poe for which I do not believe the poet is to be held responsible. These are: (1) "The Three Meetings"; (2) "The Skeleton Hand" and "The Magician"; (3) "To Sarah";

[1] See his edition of Poe's poems, p. lxii.

[2] *Poe's Works*, VII, 238 f.

[3] Cf. also *Notes and Queries*, 3d series, VII, 61 f. (January 21, 1865). Here also may be mentioned several poems published in 1821 in a Baltimore volume, *Miscellaneous Selections and Original Pieces in Prose and Verse*, edited by Elizabeth Chase. These are signed "Edgar," and it has been suggested that they are among the poems which Poe claimed to have written in 1821–1822 (see Catalogue 344 of the Merwin-Clayton Sales Company, p. 32, New York, 1910). They are described, however, in the volume in which they appear, as having been written by a youth of eighteen, whereas Poe in 1821 was only twelve. Moreover, one of the pieces (pp. 216 f.) is addressed to a sister, "Ellen," whereas Poe had but one sister, — Rosalie.

(4) "An Enigma"; (5) "A Poetical Epistle to Mr. Pickwick" and "A Bachelor's Address to his Cane"; (6) "The Times"; (7) "The Departed"; (8) "Gratitude."

(1) "The Three Meetings" is ascribed to Poe by Mr. Irving T. Richards in an article entitled "A New Poe Poem" published in *Modern Language Notes* for March, 1927.[1] Mr. Richards holds that these lines, which were published in John Neal's *Yankee and Boston Literary Gazette* in February, 1828, and which are there signed "Edgar," are an early poem of Poe's, though he suggests that they had probably been tinkered with by someone else before being sent to Neal. I find nothing in "The Three Meetings," however, whether in matter or in style, that suggests the hand of Poe. Besides, the lines are dated "Cambridge, Feb. 19, 1828," whereas (as Mr. Richards concedes) Poe was stationed at Charleston, South Carolina, at that time.

(2) "The Skeleton Hand" and "The Magician" were first attributed to Poe by Professor Harrison in 1902 on the grounds that they were subscribed with the initial "P."[2] — a signature which Poe had used with occasional articles in the *Messenger, Burton's Gentleman's Magazine,* and the *Broadway Journal* — and that they were published in the *Yankee* shortly after excerpts from his "Fairy-Land" and other early verses had appeared there. But neither of the poems is in Poe's manner; and one of them — "The

[1] XLII, 158 f.   [2] *Poe's Works*, VII, 252 f.

Magician" — is an obvious imitation of "The Ancient Mariner," whereas Poe in his acknowledged productions displayed little if anything of Coleridge's influence before 1831. The evidence of the signature, furthermore, is by no means conclusive, since there were numerous other articles in the American periodicals of the time that bore the signature "P." [1]

(3) "To Sarah" was first attributed to Poe in 1911 by Mr. J. H. Whitty. [2] It was published in the *Southern Literary Messenger* for August, 1835, [3] while Poe was connected with that magazine, and was signed "Sylvio." Mr. Whitty attributes the poem to Poe on the basis of a memorandum which he believes was made by Poe in the "Duane" copy of the *Southern Literary Messenger*, on the strength of which he also

---

[1] There are two poems in the *Token* (published at Boston) in 1829 and one in 1830 that are signed "P." but are obviously not Poe's; there are three poems bearing this signature in the Boston *Memorial* for 1826 that we can also be sure are not his; there are two poems and two prose pieces in the *American Monthly Magazine* (published at Boston) for 1830 that are surely not Poe's; and there were poems published in the Philadelphia *Casket* (May, 1827, p. 198) and in the Baltimore *Emerald* (June 21 and 28, 1828) that are subscribed with his initial but are manifestly not from his pen. Among other items signed "P." that I have stumbled upon in the periodicals of Poe's time are a dreary poem on "Ambition" in the Providence *Literary Journal* for February 22, 1834; a sonnet (without title) in the *New England Magazine* for December, 1834; "Lines" in the Philadelphia *Casket* for November, 1837; "The Fairy Queen" and "Impromptu" in *Alexander's Weekly Messenger* for December 13 and 20, 1837; "Autumn Morning" in the Philadelphia *Saturday Courier* for October 15, 1842; "Woman's Tactics" in the *New Mirror* for July 8, 1843; and "To —— (On Giving Her an Album)" in the *Dollar Newspaper* for May 17, 1848. See, too, my note below (p. 235) on the lines "To Mary" in the *New England Magazine* for January, 1832.

[2] *Poe's Poems*, pp. 142, 286.   [3] I, 692.

attributes to Poe a story, "The Doom," which was published in the same number of the *Messenger*. But, as I shall later show,[1] Mr. Whitty is mistaken in attributing "The Doom" to Poe. Besides, in both mood and diction the lines "To Sarah" are unlike anything we have that is indubitably Poe's. Particularly unlike Poe is the very realistic reference to the mocking-bird in the second stanza; and unlike him also is the slip (in the third stanza) in referring to "Hermon's dew" as "Hermia's dew," an allusion which Poe gets quite right both in *Politian* and in his lines to Mrs. Shew beginning "Not long ago, the writer of these lines." [2]

(4) Another poem first attributed to Poe by Mr. Whitty [3] is "An Enigma," some lines which were cited in a brief note — apparently by Poe — entitled "Palindromes" in *Burton's Gentleman's Magazine* for May, 1840, as furnishing an example of "an enigma where all the words required are palindromes." The writer of this note, however, does not set up a claim to the authorship of the poem. Moreover, if the poem actually be Poe's, it was written by him a good many years before its publication in *Burton's*; for a version of it, differing only in phrasing here and there, appeared in the Philadelphia *Casket* for May, 1827.[4] This earlier version — which is en-

[1] *Infra*, pp. 210 f.
[2] *Politian*, ed. Mabbott, p. 14; *Poe's Works*, VII, 106.
[3] *Poe's Poems*, pp. 146, 287.
[4] II, 199.

titled "Enigma" and was unsigned — runs as follows:

> First take a word that does silence proclaim,
> Which backwards and forwards does still spell the same;
> Then add to the first a feminine name,
> Which backwards and forwards does still spell the same;
> An instrument, too, which lawyers oft frame,
> And backwards and forwards does still spell the same;
> A very rich fruit whose Botanical name,
> Both backwards and forwards does still spell the same;
> And a musical note which all will proclaim,
> Both backwards and forwards does still spell the same;
> The initials of these, when joined form a name,
> Which every young lady that's married will claim,
> And backwards and forwards does still spell the same.

(5) The two pieces of doggerel entitled "A Poetical Epistle to Mr. Pickwick" and "A Bachelor's Address to his Cane," embodied in a volume entitled *English Notes* [1] (published at Boston in 1842), were first attributed to Poe by Mr. Joseph Jackson in an article in the *World's Work* for January, 1912.[2] As I point out below, the inadequacy of the evidence on which *English Notes* has been attributed to Poe is conclusively shown by Mr. W. N. C. Carlton in an article in the *Americana Collector* for February, 1926.[3] With the rejection of *English Notes* as Poe's, the case for Poe's authorship of these two effusions falls to the ground.

---

[1] *English Notes*, ed. Lewis M. Thompson, New York, 1920, pp. 154 f., 157 f.

[2] XXIII, 292.   [3] *Infra*, pp. 224 f.

(6) "The Times," also a piece of doggerel, was published in the Boston *Mail* for January 11, 1843, where it is ascribed to "The Author of 'English Notes.'" [1] The rejection of *English Notes* as Poe's automatically carries with it the rejection of these lines.

(7) "The Departed," published in the *Broadway Journal* for July 12, 1845, above the initial "L.," has been ascribed to Poe by the poet Chivers; [2] but as I have elsewhere tried to show, [3] the poem is probably the work of Chivers himself.

(8) "Gratitude," attributed to Poe by Mr. Whitty, [4] first appeared in *The Symposia* published at Providence, Rhode Island, early in 1845, above the initials "E. A. P." The lines do not resemble anything that has been authenticated as Poe's. There appeared in *The Symposia*, moreover, two items signed with the initials "E. A. B.," which begets the suspicion that the initials "E. A. P." as appended to the poem involve a typographical error for "E. A. B.," the initials of the Boston poet and artist E. A. Brackett, author of *Twilight Hours* and other volumes.

There are also a number of poems that have been ascribed to Poe on evidence that is more or less plausible, but that is not entirely convincing. These include: (1) "Oh Tempora! oh Mores!" some crude

---

[1] See Miss Mary E. Phillips, *Poe — the Man*, pp. 738 f.

[2] See the *Waverley Magazine* for July 30, 1853 (p. 73).

[3] Cf. the University of Texas *Studies in English*, No. 10, pp. 152 f. (1930). But see also the *American Book Collector*, II, 233 (October, 1932), for the suggestion that the poem was written by J. Hunt, Jr.

[4] *Poe's Poems*, pp. 144 f., 286 f.

verses published in the *No Name Magazine* for October, 1889; (2) "Lines to Louisa," a short poem, possibly in Poe's handwriting, found among the Ellis-Allan Papers; (3) "Alone," some lines preserved in manuscript in a Baltimore autograph album; (4) "A West Point Lampoon," said to have been written by Poe while a cadet at West Point; (5) two poems — "To ——" ("Sleep on," etc.) and "Fanny" — published in the Baltimore *Saturday Visiter* in 1833 above the signature "Tamerlane"; (6) "Spiritual Song," a fragment of three lines found in manuscript, conjecturally in Poe's autograph, in the desk used by the poet while editor of the *Southern Literary Messenger*; (7) "The Great Man," also from a manuscript found in Poe's desk; (8) "Extract from an Unfinished Poem," published anonymously in the *Southern Literary Messenger* for March, 1835; (9) "Ballad," published anonymously in the *Messenger* for August, 1835; (10) "Fragment of a Campaign Song," published in the New York *Times* of March 4, 1899; (11) "New Year's Address of the Carriers of the Columbia Spy," published in the *Spy* of January 1, 1844, and tentatively assigned to Poe by Mr. T. O. Mabbott; (12) "Impromptu. To Kate Carol," some punning lines that appeared in the *Broadway Journal* for April 26, 1845; and (13) "Stanzas" and "The Divine Right of Kings," published above the initial "P." in *Graham's Magazine* for October and December (respectively), 1845.[1]

[1] xxvii, 189, 251.

(1) The lines "Oh Tempora! oh Mores!" were first published in the *No Name Magazine* for October, 1889,[1] by E. L. Didier, who declared that the manuscript of the poem had long been in the possession of the MacKenzie family in Richmond, with whom Poe's sister Rosalie made her home, and that their authenticity as Poe's had been vouched for by John R. Thompson.[2] Both in style and in mood the lines are unlike anything published by Poe in his first volume of poems (1827) or in any subsequent volume; moreover, John R. Thompson, so far as I am aware, nowhere publicly attributed the poem to Poe, while Didier's authority is discredited by his misleading statements with respect to the poem "Alone." [3] Such evidence as we have in support of the genuineness of the poem, then, is wholly external and second-hand, and as such is far from conclusive.

(2) The poem which I have referred to as "Lines to Louisa" is a crude lyric of four stanzas found in manuscript (without title) among papers left by the firm of Ellis and Allan (of which Poe's foster-father was the junior member), and now preserved in the Library of Congress at Washington. The lines are perhaps in Poe's handwriting, though we can be by no means certain of this. In style they are clumsy and bare; and I can discover in them nothing that points to Poe's authorship. Their claim to authenticity must rest, then, on the circumstance that they

[1] I, 1.
[2] Whitty, *Poe's Poems*, p. 165 n.
[3] See *infra*, p. 204.

were found among the Ellis-Allan Papers (which are a welter of miscellaneous documents from hundreds of different hands) and the possibility that they are in Poe's handwriting, evidence that is exceedingly flimsy.

(3) "Alone," a poem much in the manner of "Tamerlane," was first published by E. L. Didier in *Scribner's Monthly* for September, 1875,[1] and was there said to have been taken from a manuscript, in Poe's handwriting, that had long been in the possession of a Baltimore family. Didier published along with the poem what he declared to be a facsimile of the manuscript, but when it was pointed out that the date and place of the poem as given in this facsimile were inaccurate, he admitted that the date and place and the title had been filled in by himself, but maintained that the rest of the facsimile was in Poe's autograph. It is fairly evident, however, that the poem proper is in the same handwriting as that of the date and place. Nevertheless, the style and diction and matter of the lyric so strongly suggest Poe that Poe's editors have, almost without exception, held the poem to be genuine. The case for Poe's authorship, in view of the internal evidence, seems to me to be strong.

(4) "A West Point Lampoon" is a squib of eight lines said to have been written by Poe while at West Point and to have been directed against one of his instructors at the Academy. The lines were first

[1] x, 608.

attributed to Poe by Henry B. Hirst in the Philadelphia *Saturday Museum* of February 25, 1843; and
as Hirst's article was made up from materials furnished him by Poe, it would seem virtually certain
that the poem is authentic. A fellow-cadet of Poe's
at the Academy, T. W. Gibson, also testifies to its
authenticity in an article published in *Harper's
Monthly* for November, 1867.[1]

(5) The two poems "To ——" ("Sleep on, sleep
on, another hour") and "Fanny," found by Professor J. C. French in the Baltimore *Saturday Visiter*
for May, 1833, where they appear above the signature "Tamerlane,"[2] are not unlike Poe's earlier work
and may well have been youthful compositions which
he felt to be unworthy of public acknowledgment. In
particular, the third and fourth stanzas of "To ——"
seem to me to be in Poe's early manner, though both
poems in every likelihood proceeded from the same
pen. The use of the pseudonym "Tamerlane" obviously strengthens the supposition that these poems
are the work of Poe.

(6) The lines entitled "Spiritual Song," found by
Mr. Whitty in manuscript in a desk used by Poe
while editor of the *Southern Literary Messenger*,[3] are
apparently in Poe's autograph, and are, moreover,
in the manner of some of his early lyrics, especially
the songs in "Al Aaraaf." Hence they are with great

[1] xxxv, 754.
[2] *Modern Language Notes*, xxxiii, 257 f. (May, 1918).
[3] Whitty, pp. 139, 283 f.

likelihood Poe's. The evidence cannot be held to be conclusive, however, since, even though in Poe's handwriting, it is possible that the manuscript was copied by him from some other source, as happened in the case of Miss Winslow's parody of "The Raven" and in the case of the excerpt from Mrs. Osgood's "Woman's Trust." [1]

(7) "The Great Man," also found by Mr. Whitty in the desk used by Poe while editing the *Messenger*, is likewise held by him to be in Poe's handwriting.[2] The case for or against its genuineness as Poe's is, then, much the same as with "Spiritual Song," except that in style and content "The Great Man" is much less like Poe's characteristic work than is "Spiritual Song."

(8) "Extract from an Unfinished Poem" is a fragment of some thirty lines which appeared anonymously in the *Southern Literary Messenger* for March, 1835.[3] In tone and diction the lines manifestly resemble Poe's early long poem, "Tamerlane," and it may well be that they are from his scrap-bag of unfinished or rejected verses, though obviously the evidence at hand is insufficient to do more than to suggest the possibility of Poe's authorship.[4]

(9) "Ballad," first published in the *Southern Literary Messenger* for August, 1835,[5] is prefaced by a letter signed "Sidney," in which it is asserted that

---

[1] *Supra*, p. 192.   [2] See Whitty, pp. 143 f., 285 f.
[3] I, 370.
[4] See *Modern Language Notes*, XXXII, 271 f. (May, 1917).
[5] I, 705 f.

the poem was composed by a fair lady acquaintance of the editor's and had never before been printed. The lines strikingly resemble Poe's "Bridal Ballad" (with which they possess one line in common save for the variation of a single word), and Professor Woodberry has suggested that they were probably an early draft of that poem.[1] In this conjecture he is in all likelihood right. The attribution of the poem to another (in the prefatory note accompanying it in the *Messenger*) would involve a piece of mystification by the poet paralleled by his attribution (by implication) of his "Letter to B——" to another in the text of that essay published in the *Messenger* for July, 1836.[2]

(10) "Fragment of a Campaign Song" is a scrap of four lines first attributed to Poe by the artist Gabriel Harrison in the New York *Times* of March 4, 1899, and declared by him to have been written by the poet on a visit to New York in the winter of 1843–1844. In matter and style it resembles nothing else that has been associated with Poe; on the other hand, Harrison, who at one time painted a portrait of Poe, seems to have been a thoroughly reliable witness,[3] and there would accordingly appear to be little ground for doubting its authenticity.

(11) "New Year's Address of the Carriers of the Columbia Spy," published in the Columbia *Spy* of January 1, 1844, is tentatively assigned to Poe by Mr. T. O. Mabbott.[4] The poem is without distinc-

---

[1] *Life of Poe*, II, 415. [2] II, 501 f.
[3] Woodberry, II, 422 f. [4] *Doings of Gotham*, pp. 113 f.

tion, and is clumsily done; but Mr. Mabbott calls attention to certain parallels with Poe's well-authenticated work, and suggests, by way of accounting for the crudity of the lines, that they may have been written in haste or at the suggestion of the editors of the *Spy* — and for a consideration. This is possible, but the evidence in the case is almost wholly circumstantial, and hence is, at best, as Mr. Mabbott admits, inconclusive.

(12) "Impromptu. To Kate Carol," four lines originally published in the *Broadway Journal* of April 26, 1845,[1] as a part of the "Editorial Miscellany" for that issue, was first attributed to Poe by Mr. Whitty.[2] The bulk of the editorials appearing in the *Broadway* at this time were evidently the work of Poe. Besides, as Mr. Whitty notes, "Kate Carol" was a pen-name adopted by Mrs. Frances Sargent Osgood with a number of her contributions to the magazines of the forties,[3] and Poe, as we know, was openly coquetting with Mrs. Osgood at the time. Hence there is much likelihood that the lines proceeded from him.

(13) "Stanzas" and "The Divine Right of Kings," first assigned to Poe by Mr. Whitty in an article in the New York *Sun* for November 21, 1915, were published in *Graham's Magazine* for October and December (respectively), 1845, above the signature

[1] I, 271.   [2] *Poems of Poe*, p. 287.
[3] Among them the *Union Magazine* and *Labree's Illustrated Magazine*. See also a statement of Griswold's confirming Mr. Whitty's statement in *Laurel Leaves*, New York, 1854, p. 22.

"P." [1] This signature is expanded, so Mr. Whitty informs us, in a copy of *Graham's* once owned by Mrs. Osgood, to read "E. A. P." Neither of the two poems, however, resembles very closely anything else that has been attributed to Poe; and the inadequacy of the evidence afforded by the signature "P." is apparent.[2] Inadequate also, as I have already shown,[3] is the handwriting as a basis of unqualified ascription of authorship. Further evidence must be forthcoming, then, before we can be sure that these two poems are Poe's.[4]

(*B*) *Tales.* — Of the tales that have at some time been associated with Poe's name, there are only four about the authenticity of which any doubt still remains.[5] These are (1) "A Dream," published in the Philadelphia *Saturday Evening Post* for August 13, 1831; (2) "The Doom," published in the *Southern Literary Messenger* for January, 1835; (3) "Erostratus," published in the *Southern Literary Messenger* for July, 1836; and (4) "Who is the Mur-

[1] XXVII, 189, 251.
[2] See my note on "The Skeleton Hand" and "The Magician," pp. 197 f., above.
[3] *Supra*, p. 192.
[4] Two of Poe's early poems, "The Happiest Day" and "Dreams," it should be added, were published, as Mr. Mabbott has pointed out (*Poe's Brother*, New York, 1926, pp. 42 f., 49 f.), above the initials of Poe's brother, William Henry Poe, in the Baltimore *North American* in 1827. But Mr. Mabbott questions whether William Henry Poe actually had any hand in their composition.
[5] Professor Woodberry informs us (I, 134 n.) that the late W. M. Griswold inclined to attribute to Poe, "on internal evidence solely," four stories published in *Godey's Lady's Book* in 1833–1834, but he rightly concludes that there is no good ground for believing these to be Poe's.

derer?" published in *Blackwood's Magazine* for May, 1842.[1]

(1) "A Dream" was published in the *Saturday Evening Post* for August 13, 1831, and is there signed with the initial "P." For the suggestion that it is possibly the work of Poe, I am myself responsible.[2] In mood and diction the story is not unlike some of the more gruesome of Poe's early tales; besides, Poe's friend and comrade, L. A. Wilmer, was at the time on the staff of the *Post*, and it was through his influence perhaps that two of Poe's poems, his "Sonnet. To Science" and the lines "To Helen," had shortly before [3] been published in that journal. But such evidence as we have is plainly insufficient to do more than to raise the question whether the story is not the work of Poe.

(2) "The Doom," a brief narrative published in the *Southern Literary Messenger* for January, 1835,[4] and there signed "Benedict," is attributed to Poe by Mr. J. H. Whitty on the basis of a memorandum

---

[1] A story entitled "The Ghost of a Grey Tadpole," originally published in the Baltimore *Republican and Argus* of February 1, 1844, and there attributed to Poe, has recently been shown by Mr. T. O. Mabbott (*American Irish Historical Society*, xxix, 121 f. [1931]) to be the work of Thomas Dunn English. So, also, a crude tale entitled "La Canción de Hollands" published in Spanish in *La América* for October 28, 1883, and there represented as being a translation of a story by Poe, has been convincingly shown, by John E. Englekirk, Jr., in the *New Mexico Quarterly*, i, 247 f. (August, 1931), to be a hoax at Poe's expense. The author of the hoax, so Mr. Englekirk plausibly suggests (p. 261), was Aurélien Scholl.

[2] See *Modern Language Notes*, xxxii, 271 (May, 1917).

[3] In its issues of September 11, 1830, and May 21, 1831, respectively.

[4] i, 235 f.

which he believes to have been made by the poet in the "Duane" copy of the *Messenger* for 1835.[1] In style and workmanship the story is exceedingly crude; in fact, it is so poor a performance that the editor of the *Messenger* took occasion, at the end of the number in which it appeared, to apologize for its admission into his columns.[2] The only evidence in support of Poe's authorship is, then, the memorandum in the "Duane" *Messenger*. There is, to be sure, a reference at one point in the story to Poe's well-known swimming feat in the James;[3] but this, in my judgment, tells against Poe's authorship rather than for it. In a letter in the issue of the *Messenger* for May, 1835,[4] it may be added, Poe comments on the allusion made to him in the story, and in a later letter he inquires of Mr. White, proprietor of the *Messenger*, as to the authorship of the story.[5] Had Poe actually been the author of the tale, it is all but inconceivable that this correspondence could have gone on without White's discovering it.[6]

(3) The first to suggest that Poe perhaps wrote the

---

[1] *Poe's Poems*, pp. xxviii, 286.

[2] The *Southern Literary Messenger*, I, 254 f.

[3] *Ibid.*, p. 235.   [4] *Ibid.*, p. 468.   [5] *Poe's Works*, XVII, 10.

[6] Evidence is also at hand of another sort discrediting the theory of Poe's authorship. In the Richmond *Compiler* of April 8, 1835, there appeared a letter from a correspondent who signs himself "The Writer of the Doom," replying hotly to a criticism of "The Doom" that had appeared in the *Compiler* two days before. The writer of this reply represents himself as writing from Richmond on April 6. But there is no record of Poe's making a trip to Richmond in April, 1835; on the contrary, there is every reason to believe that he was still in Baltimore at that time, where he was living in poverty. What Mr. Whitty takes to be an acknowledg-

tale "Erostratus" [1] was B. B. Minor in his volume *The Southern Literary Messenger*.[2] Miss Alterton also suggests [3] the possibility of Poe's authorship, her grounds for associating the story with Poe being the classic setting with which the plot has to do and sundry classical allusions that are introduced into the story. Poe was a staunch believer in the classics, and he seems to have been especially interested in classical lore during the time of his connection with the *Messenger*. He published in the *Messenger* for August of the same year his "Pinakidia," [4] a collection of cullings in the manner of Disraeli, a good many of which are from the classics, and he introduced catalogues of classical authors into several of his early stories.[5] But Lucian Minor, as I have already shown,[6] was also connected with the *Messenger* at this time, and he was more immediately interested in the classics than was Poe. Besides, the style of the story is more bare, more metallic, I think, than Poe's; and the incidents of the narrative are but little elaborated; so that I cannot bring myself to believe that this story was the work of Poe.

(4) The story "Who is the Murderer?" [7] is as-

ment by Poe of the authorship of "The Doom" is, I should guess, a notation relating to the reference made to his swimming feat.

[1] The *Southern Literary Messenger*, II, 467 f. (July, 1836).
[2] New York, 1905, p. 49.
[3] *Origins of Poe's Critical Theory*, p. 107.
[4] The *Southern Literary Messenger*, II, 573 f. (August, 1836).
[5] *Poe's Works*, II, 38 f., 142, 326.
[6] *Supra*, p. 194.
[7] *Blackwood's Magazine*, LI, 553-578 (May, 1842).

signed to Poe by Miss Mary E. Phillips [1] on the supposition that it is one of the articles which Poe claimed to have written for British journals early in the forties.[2] The story has Poe's circumstantiality, and the method adopted in presenting the testimony of the witnesses in the trial that is described is not unlike that adopted in "The Murders in the Rue Morgue." But the tale is much more loosely constructed than was usual with Poe, especially in his better years, and the suspense and the climax are poorly managed. Besides, it seems to me very unlikely that Poe would have referred to Kit North as "dear Christopher" and "your loving friend," [3] as does the writer of this article.[4]

(*C*) *Book-Reviews, Editorials, and Miscellaneous Prose Items.* — Among book-reviews attributed to Poe either erroneously or on evidence that is inconclusive are the following: [5]

[1] *Poe — the Man*, p. 712.

[2] *Poe's Works*, I, 346; Woodberry, I, 220.

[3] *Blackwood's*, LI, 578.

[4] The suggestion is made by Allen and Mabbott in their volume *Poe's Brother* (New York, 1926, p. 53) that Poe wrote, "at least in part," the story entitled "The Pirate" contributed by Poe's brother, William Henry Poe, to the Baltimore *North American* for November 27, 1827.

[5] There are also certain items once assigned to Poe that have already been rejected as his. Among these are:

(1) A notice of "Glenn's Reply to the Critics" in *Burton's Gentleman's Magazine* for September, 1839 (V, 164 f.). This is given to Poe in the list of his writings printed in *Poe's Works*, XVI, 363, but, as was pointed out in the *Nation* of December 23, 1909 (p. 623), it was written by Burton.

(2) A review of *The Poems of Alfred Tennyson* in *Graham's* for September, 1842 (XXI, 152 f.). This appears in *Poe's Works*, XI, 127 f. It has been denied to Poe, on the basis of internal evidence, by Mr. J. H.

(1) A notice of Bryant's poems in the *Southern Literary Messenger* for January, 1835.[1] This is given to Poe by implication in a bibliographical note in the Stedman-Woodberry edition of *Poe's Works*,[2] and it is included in the collective edition of *Poe's Works*[3] by Professor Harrison, though the editor expresses doubts as to its authenticity.[4] Poe contributed to the *Messenger* as early as February, 1835,[5] but I know of nothing to indicate that he wrote for the *Messenger* before that time. The article in question, moreover, is less simple and forthright than is usual with Poe, and is more florid in style.

(2) A paragraph of five lines on "The Unities" in the *Southern Literary Messenger* for August, 1835.[6] This item, a paraphrase of a paragraph from Schlegel's *Lectures on Dramatic Art*, is assigned to Poe by Whitty (the New York *Times*, December 11, 1909). In a review of Griswold's anthology published in the *Saturday Museum* in 1843 (*Poe's Works*, XI, 237 f.), the review is attributed to Griswold.

(3) A number of translations from the French published in the *New Mirror* in 1843–1844 above the signature "E. P." and attributed to Poe by Ingram (p. 201). These, as Professor Woodberry has shown (II, 103), came from the pen of a woman, — probably, as he suggests, Emily Percival. A poem — "The Idiot Boy" — bearing the same signature and published in *Graham's Magazine* for June, 1847 (XXX, 330 f.), probably came from the same source.

Two other spurious items are listed by Charles F. Heartman and Kenneth Rede in their *Census of First Editions and Source Materials by Edgar Allan Poe in American Collections*, Metuchen, New Jersey, 1932, I, pp. 63 f., 66 f., — namely, *The Philosophy of Animal Magnetism*, Philadelphia, 1837, and *A Chapter in the History of Vivum-Ovo*, Memphis, 1882.

[1] I, 250 f.   [2] VI, 324.
[3] VIII, i f.   [4] *Poe's Works*, VIII, vii n.
[5] See the *Nation*, October 19, 1911, p. 362.
[6] I, 698.

Miss Alterton in her thesis *Origins of Poe's Critical Theory* (p. 73). As Miss Alterton notes, Poe seems to have been reading Schlegel at the time, and it was like him to paraphrase his original. The paragraph is in all likelihood Poe's.

(3) A letter signed "X. Y." published in the *Southern Literary Messenger* for January, 1835.[1] This item is provisionally ascribed to Poe by Miss Alterton [2] on the basis of circumstantial evidence. The sentiments recorded are such as might have proceeded from Poe, but the style is hardly Poe's, in my opinion. Besides, "X. Y.," who represents himself as being a "purveyor" of manuscripts for the *Messenger*, caters, as he tells us, to Virginians, not (as was the case with Poe at the time) to Marylanders. I see no good reason for assigning this item to Poe.

(4) Three articles entitled "Translation" (containing a versified rendering of one of the odes of Horace), "The Classics," and "Some Ancient Greek Authors," published in the *Southern Literary Messenger* for January, March, and April, 1836,[3] respectively. These are tentatively ascribed to Poe by Miss Alterton [4] on the ground that they deal with subjects in which Poe is known to have been interested at the time.[5] Each of them is possibly Poe's; but it seems to me much more likely that they are the work of Lucian Minor, who was confessedly re-

---

[1] I, 255 f.   [2] Pp. 56 f.
[3] II, 93, 221 f., 301 f.   [4] Pp. 107, 118 f.
[5] The third of these items is also ascribed to Poe by B. B. Minor (*The Southern Literary Messenger*, p. 42).

sponsible for the translation of the "Hymn in Honor of Harmodius and Aristogiton," published in the *Southern Literary Messenger* for December, 1835,[1] and there entitled "Greek Song." There is nothing that suggests Poe, moreover, in the style of any of these articles, though it may be that Poe wrote the prose comments which accompany them.

(5) "Chief Justice Marshall," an article containing a review of three books dealing with Marshall, published in the *Messenger* for February, 1836.[2] This is given to Poe by Miss Alterton (p. 50), mainly on the ground of a reference by Poe in one of his letters [3] to an article on Marshall that he had sent to T. W. White, proprietor of the *Messenger*. The circumstantial evidence supporting Poe's authorship seems to me to have weight; but the article is largely a compilation, and is less deftly mortised together than was usual with Poe. Besides, it was not like Poe to document quite so freely his reviews as is done in this instance. It is more probable, I think, as B. B. Minor suggests,[4] that the article was written by Judge Beverly Tucker.

(6) An essay on "Genius" in the *Southern Literary Messenger* for April, 1836.[5] This is attributed to Poe by Dr. J. W. Robertson [6] and also by Miss Alterton.[7] The essay is concerned mainly with the "incompati-

---

[1] II, 38.   [2] II, 181 f.   [3] *Poe's Works*, XVII, 12.
[4] *The Southern Literary Messenger*, p. 39.
[5] II, 297 f.
[6] *Poe: A Study*, pp. 251 f.
[7] *Origins of Poe's Critical Theory*, pp. 97 f.

bility" between "poetical and philosophical genius,"
a theme with which, in one or another of its aspects,
Poe was fond of dallying. With the incompatibility
(as he held) between poetry and science he had dealt
both in his "Sonnet. To Science" and in his long
poem "Al Aaraaf." [1] And he touches on the relation
between poetry and science in his "Letter to B——"
and incidentally in "The Purloined Letter." [2] The
subject, then, is one that would have been congenial
to Poe. Two citations are made from Byron, moreover, besides quotations from Locke and Bacon,
which would argue in favor of Poe's authorship. On
the other hand, three quotations are taken from
Lucretius, whom Poe very rarely refers to; and the
style of the paper has less of point and decision than
we ordinarily find with Poe. I doubt, then, the authenticity of this item.

(7) "Verbal Criticisms," a series of comments on
current phrases and idioms, published in the *Messenger* for May, 1836. [3] The item is attributed to Poe
by Miss Alterton (p. 100 n.) on the ground that it
appeared in the *Messenger*, and without any signature, while Poe was the editor. The article is not improbably Poe's, though it cannot be taken for granted
that all unsigned articles that appeared in the *Messenger* during his editorship are the work of his hand.
The references to Coleridge's *Table Talk* and Irving's
Tour of the Prairies point to Poe's authorship, as does

---

[1] *Poe's Works*, VII, 22, 35.   [2] *Ibid.*, VII, xxxviii f.; VI, 43.
[3] *Southern Literary Messenger*, II, 388 f.

also the comment on the use of "directly" for "as soon as," which Poe was to object to in an installment of the "Marginalia"[1] in the *Democratic Review* for December, 1844.[2] But over against the supposition of Poe's authorship it is to be noted that another idiom objected to here, the progressive passive (as "is being built"), is also objected to in a similar article published in the *Messenger* for May, 1837,[3] which seems to have proceeded from another hand than Poe's.

(8) "Character of Coriolanus," an article published in the *Southern Literary Messenger* for November, 1836,[4] and subscribed with the initial "P." This article Miss Alterton (p. 107) declares to be "unmistakably Poe's." The presence of Poe's initial at the end of the article has weight, it must be admitted; but, as has already been shown,[5] it is by no means definitive as establishing Poe's authorship. The article was perhaps written by Poe; though I do not feel that we can be sure of this.

(9) Three articles entitled "The Philosophy of Antiquity," published in the *Southern Literary Messenger* for November, 1836, and January and February, 1837.[6] These are provisionally ascribed to Poe by Miss Alterton (pp. 107, 110). Poe was interested in philosophy, as his writings reveal at various points; but I can find nothing either in the content or in the

---

[1] *Poe's Works*, xvi, 43.
[2] xv, 586.
[3] iii, 334 f.
[4] ii, 737 f.
[5] *Supra*, p. 198 n.
[6] ii, 739 f.; iii, 32 f., 158.

style of these papers that serves to establish their authenticity as his.

(10) Certain reviews published in the *Southern Literary Messenger* for the months of February, April, October, and November, 1837, conjecturally ascribed to Poe by myself on the strength of a letter of his to Mrs. Sarah Josepha Hale, of the date October 20, 1837, in the course of which he asserts that he was at the time acting as editor of the *Messenger*.[1] Miss Mary E. Phillips in her *Poe — the Man* (p. 541) has suggested that Poe's letter to Mrs. Hale was misdated by him, and that it was actually written on October 30, 1836; and she cites in support of her suggestion the fact that Mrs. Hale's *The Ladies' Wreath*, to which reference is made in Poe's letter, was copyrighted in 1836, a circumstance that I first discovered some time after the publication of my article. This circumstance makes it likely, I think, that the items that I had provisionally assigned to Poe are the work of some other hand or hands.[2]

(11) "New Views of the Solar System," published in the *Southern Literary Messenger* for July and December, 1838,[3] and "New Views of the Tides," published in the *Messenger* for December, 1838.[4]

[1] See the New York *Nation*, LXXXIX, 9 f. (July 1, 1909).

[2] It should be noted, however, that a second edition of *The Ladies' Wreath*, "improved and enlarged," appeared at Boston in 1839, and it is barely possible that Poe's reference is to this second edition, then (on this supposition) in process of compilation and revision, but delayed in publication until a year or more later.

[3] IV, 433 f., 769 f.   [4] IV, 747 f.

Miss Alterton holds (p. 144) that these articles are possibly Poe's. But I know of nothing to indicate that Poe had any connection with the *Messenger* in 1838; on the contrary, there is evidence to show that he believed himself to be *persona non grata* to the proprietor of the *Messenger* (T. W. White) at that time.[1]

(12) "Half an Hour in the Academy of Fine Arts at Philadelphia," published in *Burton's Gentleman's Magazine* for August, 1839.[2] This article is attributed to Poe by Miss Alterton (p. 93), on the theory that it represents some of the miscellaneous material which Poe claims to have written for *Burton's*, but for which his editors have not accounted.[3] The article is professedly the work of "A Philadelphian," whereas it would hardly have been like Poe to proclaim himself a Philadelphian. Besides, it is not, I think, in Poe's manner,[4] and it contains no phrase or allusion that one would readily associate with Poe.[5]

(13) A review of Captain Marryat's *Diary in*

---

[1] See a letter from James E. Heath to Poe, *Poe's Works*, xvii, 48.

[2] v, 78 f.　　　　　　　　[3] *Poe's Works*, i, 165.

[4] I cannot imagine Poe having spoken of a picture as "a darling picture . . . the darling'st of the darling kind": see p. 81 of the article in question.

[5] Ingram (p. 138) assigns to Poe unconditionally and Woodberry (i, 198) mentions as possibly Poe's *A Synopsis of Natural History*, "Translated from . . . Lemmonnier . . . with Additions from . . . Cuvier" (and others), reviewed by Poe in *Burton's* for July, 1839 (v, 61 f.), and there attributed to Thomas Wyatt. Poe asserts in the course of his review that he writes from "personal knowledge, and the closest inspection and collation," which would suggest the possibility that he had collaborated with Wyatt in making up the volume, as he had done earlier in the year in the composition of his *Conchologist's First Book*. So, too, Lowell in

America, published in *Burton's Gentleman's Maga-zine* for February, 1840.[1] This is listed by Professor Harrison [2] among Poe's writings, but is not included by him in the text of his edition. There is neither internal nor external evidence to support the ascrip-tion of the item to Poe. Moreover, in a letter [3] of Poe's to Burton in which he professes to give an accurate reckoning of his contributions to *Burton's* month by month, he claims to have furnished only twelve pages of original matter for the issue of Febru-ary, 1840, or precisely the number of pages covered by four items published in that issue that are all manifestly Poe's, namely, the chapter from "Julius Rodman," "The Business Man," and the reviews of *Voices of the Night* and Duncan's *Sacred Philosophy of the Seasons.*

(14) A brief review of Ainsworth's *Tower of Lon-don* in *Graham's* for March, 1841.[4] The grounds for doubting Poe's authorship of this item are these: that Poe in reviewing Ainsworth's *Guy Fawkes* in *Graham's* for November, 1841,[5] asserts that he had hitherto read nothing of *The Tower of London* save "some detached passages"; that he expresses in his notice of *Guy Fawkes* a view of Ainsworth's *Jack Sheppard* at variance with that expressed by the re-

his sketch of Poe in *Graham's* for February, 1845 (XXVII, 53), attributed the item to Poe, and we know that Lowell's sketch had passed under Poe's eye. But I have not seen a copy of this book, and so speak with diffidence about it.

[1] VI, 103, 105.   [2] *Poe's Works*, XVI, 364.
[3] Of date June 1, 1840: see Ingram, p. 143.
[4] XVIII, 142; *Poe's Works*, X, 110 f.   [5] *Ibid.*, p. 219.

viewer of *The Tower of London*; and that the reviewer
of *The Tower of London* mentions a notice by himself
of *Jack Sheppard*, whereas there is no evidence that
Poe ever published such a review.

(15) The review of G. P. R. James's *The Ancient
Régime* in *Graham's Magazine* for October, 1841.[1]
This was attributed to Poe by myself [2] on the basis
of a reference to Poe's review of James's *Corse de
Leon* in *Graham's* for June, 1841; but a foot-note
(which I had overlooked) in this issue of *Graham's*
(p. 189) gives the information that Poe wrote none
of the reviews contained in the June number.

(16) Several articles published either anonymously or pseudonymously in *Blackwood's* during the
years 1842 and 1847 and attributed to Poe by Miss
Mary E. Phillips,[3] — namely, "The Copyright Question," "Copyright," a review of Dickens's *American
Notes*, signed "Q. Q. Q.," "Maga in America,"
"The American Library," and "Emerson." [4] That
Poe wrote for *Blackwood's* is indicated by a statement
that he made in a letter to Dr. J. E. Snodgrass of
September 11, 1839, to the effect that he had recently
"made a profitable engagement with Blackwood's." [5]
He declared, too, in an autobiographical memoran-
dum sent to Griswold in 1841 that he had "lately . . .
written articles continuously for two British jour-

---

[1] xix, 190.   [2] The *Nation*, December 23, 1909, p. 623.
[3] *Poe — the Man*, pp. 591 f., 712, 719, 734, 751, 1196, 1230, 1236.
[4] These appeared in *Blackwood's* for January, May, and December,
1842, and October, November, and December, 1847, respectively.
[5] Woodberry, I, 220.

nals." [1] Miss Phillips, then, is entitled to our gratitude for endeavoring to clear up the mystery surrounding Poe's alleged contributions to British periodicals. But I am not convinced that any one of the articles that she mentions was written by Poe. I can find in no one of them anything that smacks of Poe's characteristic style, — except, perhaps, in the article entitled "The Copyright Question," which has the intensity and the precision that distinguish Poe's work. But the copyright question was an important question, and it seems to me unlikely that the editor of *Blackwood's* would have commissioned a writer as little known as Poe was in 1842 to prepare for him a lengthy article on the subject. Poe's authorship of the article on *American Notes* is discredited, among other things, by the statement [2] that Dickens was "justly oppressed and disgusted at the consciousness of being in a slave country." Similarly the article on "Emerson" is discredited as Poe's by the statement, twice made (pp. 644, 657), that Emerson displayed "above all others" in America "undoubted marks of original genius," — a view that runs quite counter to Poe's recorded judgments on Emerson. And the article on "The American Library" was apparently written by an Englishman, — certainly not by Poe, for he constantly misspells the name of Simms, and he professes to be uncertain as to whether Margaret Fuller should be referred to as "Mrs." or "Miss."

[1] *Poe's Works*, I, 346. [2] *Blackwood's*, CII, p. 793.

(17) The article entitled "Imagination" (a review of Louisa Frances Poulter's *Imagination*) published in *Graham's* for March, 1842.[1] Professor Harrison lists this — perhaps by an oversight — in his bibliography of Poe,[2] but he does not include it in his edition. In the table of contents for the volume of *Graham's* in which the article appeared, it is ascribed to Park Benjamin.

(18) A review of Bulwer's *Zanoni* in *Graham's* for June, 1842.[3] That this review is not Poe's is established by a letter written by him to J. E. Snodgrass of June 4, 1842,[4] in which Poe makes a vigorous denial of its authorship. Poe asserts in the same place that it was not from the pen of Griswold, but was the "handiwork of some underling."

(19) A review of Griswold's *Poets and Poetry of America*, also in *Graham's* for June, 1842.[5] This article is included in the Harrison edition of Poe;[6] but it does not appear in Griswold's edition; nor is it attributed to Poe by W. M. Griswold in his edition of his father's letters.[7] And it is not mentioned by Poe in a list of his publications about Griswold sent the latter in 1849,[8] in the hope, apparently, of placating him in advance of the publication of a forth-

[1] xx, 174 f.   [2] *Poe's Works*, xvi, 367.

[3] xx, 354 f.; *Poe's Works*, xi, 115 f.

[4] Sold at the Maier Sale in 1909, and published in Catalogue 784 of the Anderson Auction Company, pp. 210 f.

[5] xx, 356.   [6] *Poe's Works*, xi, 124 f.

[7] *Passages from the Correspondence of Rufus W. Griswold*, Cambridge, 1898.

[8] *Poe's Works*, xvii, 326.

coming edition of his anthology, in which Poe was eager to receive favorable notice. Had Poe written the review he would in all likelihood have included it in his list; for it contains nothing that is especially disparaging to Griswold. Finally, there is Poe's declaration in his letter to Snodgrass of June 4, 1842,[1] that he had withdrawn from *Graham's* with the May issue. All this makes Poe's title extremely questionable.[2]

(20) A volume entitled *English Notes* and signed "Quarles Quickens," published at Boston in 1842. The volume was first attributed to Poe by Mr. Joseph Jackson in an article published in the *World's Work* for January, 1912,[3] and it is also assigned to Poe by Miss Phillips.[4] Mr. Jackson, who brought out (with Mr. George H. Sargent) a reprint of the volume in 1920, assembles in the preface of this reprint [5] the evidence as he sees it in support of Poe's authorship, noting among other things that Poe had an axe to grind with Dickens, that he had adopted the pseudonym "Quarles" with the first publication of "The Raven," that both "Quarles Quickens" and Poe were given to making a show of erudition, that Poe was, like "Quarles Quickens," an "intense lover of

---

[1] Catalogue 784 of the Anderson Auction Company, p. 210.

[2] The denying of this item to Poe apparently necessitates also the denying to him the brief notice of Griswold's book in the May issue of *Graham's* which I assigned to him in the *Nation* of December 23, 1909 (p. 623).

[3] XXIII, 292 f. See also a further article by the same writer in the *Sewanee Review*, XXVI, 274 f. (July, 1918).

[4] *Poe — the Man*, pp. 718 f.   [5] Pp. 15 f.

America," and that Poe was acquainted with Europe. But that this volume was not the work of Poe has been pretty conclusively shown by Mr. W. N. C. Carlton in an article in the *Americana Collector* for February, 1926.[1] Mr. Carlton takes up the chief points proposed by Mr. Jackson and demonstrates their inadequacy; and by way of further confutation of the assumption of Poe's authorship, he calls attention [2] to some lines entitled "The Times" published in the Boston *Daily Mail* of January 7, 1843, and there attributed to "the Author of English Notes," lines which are, as he justly observes, sheer doggerel and may scarcely be conceived of as the work of Poe by any stretch of the imagination.

(21) An extended review of Griswold's *Poets and Poetry of America* published in the Philadelphia *Saturday Museum* early in 1843 (probably in January). The review is ascribed to Poe by W. F. Gill, who reprints it in his life of Poe.[3] Professor Woodberry holds [4] that the article is "indubitably Poe's," and his opinion in any matter relating to Poe is entitled to high respect. But I do not feel that this article may safely be assigned to Poe without reservation. The reviewer's observations on prosody, his insistence on honesty in criticism, his mention of "ideality" as a poetic trait, his praise of Willis and Thomas and Conrad and Mrs. Osgood, and his censure of Wordsworth and Keats, all point to Poe as

[1] III, 186 f. [2] Pp. 189 f.
[3] New York, 1877, pp. 327 f. [4] II, 48.

the author. But the scurrilous and egotistical tone adopted in the review, and the looseness and carelessness of style, point in the opposite direction; and so also with the characterization of Bryant (p. 223) as a poet whose "sole merit is tolerable versification and fine marches of description." [1] Moreover, in a list that Poe gave shortly before his death of the articles that he had written about Griswold,[2] he does not include this review. It is possible, of course, that Poe wrote the review in collaboration with some other contributor to the *Saturday Museum*; or it may be that he merely touched up a review that some of his admirers had submitted to him; or, again, and this seems to me the most plausible theory, it may be that Poe had no hand in the review, the article being written by some imitator of his manner, — with great likelihood, I think, the Philadelphia poetaster Henry B. Hirst.[3]

(22) "Our Magazine Literature," an article published in the *New World* for March 11, 1843,[4] and there subscribed with the letter "L." The item is attributed to Poe by W. M. Griswold in *Passages from the Correspondence of Rufus W. Griswold* (p. 118), but on what ground he does not state. In both style and substance the article is not unlike Poe's work.

---

[1] *Poe's Works*, xi, 223. The judgment is quite at variance with the judgments recorded by Poe in his known reviews of Bryant.

[2] See a letter to Griswold written at some time in 1849 (Griswold, i, xxii).

[3] As Miss Phillips (*Poe — the Man*, p. 783) has suggested. If Poe actually wrote the review, I should guess that he wrote while in his cups.

[4] vi, 302-303.

Besides, L. G. Clark, editor of the *Knickerbocker*, apparently understood the article to be Poe's, since he refers to it in the *Knickerbocker* of April, 1843,[1] as the work of an "authorling . . . of a small volume of . . . trash . . . fallen dead-born from the press, before the first fifty copies printed are exhausted in a third edition." But such evidence as we have is insufficient to warrant the unconditional ascription of the article to Poe.[2]

(23) Three editorials published in the Philadelphia *Public Ledger* in July, 1844, and ascribed to Poe by Eli Bowen, editor of the *Columbia Spy*,[3] to which journal Poe contributed a series of articles at about the same time. From these papers it appears that Bowen was in fairly close touch with Poe; hence we are justified in concluding, I think, with Mr. T. O. Mabbott,[4] that the evidence is "almost conclusive" in support of Poe's authorship.

(24) Two articles on "Puffing" and a paragraph entitled "Literary Theft" published in the *Columbia Spy* in 1844. These are provisionally attributed to Poe by Professor Mabbott, but on circumstantial evidence alone;[5] hence we must await further evi-

---

[1] xxi, 380.

[2] It should be added that in the *Broadway Journal* for July 12, 1845 (ii, 7), there appeared a poem, "The Departed," subscribed with the letter "L.," which has been attributed to Poe; but as I have already noted (*supra*, p. 201), this poem was probably the work of Thomas Holley Chivers.

[3] *Doings of Gotham*, ed. J. E. Spannuth and T. O. Mabbott, pp. 88 f.

[4] *Ibid.*, p. 88.

[5] *Ibid.*, pp. 108 f., 111.

dence before these items may be confidently assigned to Poe.

(25) An article signed "Outis" and published in the New York *Evening Mirror* of March 1, 1845,[1] in the course of the so-called "Longfellow War." The article is ascribed to Poe by Miss Mary E. Phillips, in her *Poe — the Man*,[2] on the theory that it was composed by Poe as a hoax in an effort to advertise himself in the literary world. The suggestion is an ingenious one, but, as I have elsewhere tried to show,[3] there is no direct evidence to support it, and circumstantial evidence, also, seems to me to tell strongly against it.[4] The article was universally accepted at the time as the work of one of Longfellow's admirers, and I can find nothing in it, either in matter or in style, to beget doubts of its sincerity.

(26) "A Reviewer Reviewed," an article preserved in Poe's handwriting but purporting to be from the pen of one "Walter G. Bowen," first published in the New York *Journal* for March 15, 1896. The article has been attributed to Poe both by Professor George E. Woodberry (on the strength of its existing in Poe's autograph)[5] and by Miss Mary E.

[1] Reprinted in *Poe's Works*, XII, 46 f.
[2] II, 956 f.
[3] University of Texas *Studies in English*, No. 8, pp. 107 f. (1928).
[4] I am aware that Miss Phillips cites in support of her theory the article "A Reviewer Reviewed," which she believes to have been written by Poe and to have been conceived likewise as a hoax, but while this evidence is not without weight, it seems to me insufficient to offset the evidence pointing in the opposite direction.
[5] The New York *Journal*, March 15, 1896.

Phillips.[1] It would seem to me improbable that Poe would have written a criticism that is so frankly condemnatory of himself as this. Besides, as I have shown above,[2] it is unsafe to assign an item to Poe on the strength of its being preserved in his autograph. But the argument on this score has less of weight in the present instance since the manuscript runs to several pages. There are, furthermore, certain details in the article, as the mention of Poe's exceptional powers of analysis, the reference to Tupper's review of the *Tales*, and the assertion that "The Sleeper" and "Dream-Land" are superior as poetry to "The Raven," that indubitably suggest the hand of Poe. Hence, although the evidence is inconclusive, I am inclined to believe that the article is a freakish production of Poe's, which, however, it seems that he never completed and which he never saw fit to publish.

There are also a good many other reviews and book-notices that have been attributed to Poe that have not been completely established as authentic. On the basis of a rather comprehensive general statement made by the poet (in the fall of 1836) concerning the book-reviews that had appeared in the *Southern Literary Messenger* Harrison assigns to him the entire list of these reviews.[3] But Poe's statement—"Since

[1] *Poe — the Man*, pp. 959, 968.

[2] See above, p. 192.

[3] *Poe's Works*, VIII, X, XVI. Poe evidently counted the Sigourney-Gould-Ellet review in the issue for January, 1836, as three items, and the Drake-Halleck review in the issue for April as two items (see Poe's own statement, *ibid.*, p. xiv).

the commencement of my editorship in December last ninety-four books have been reviewed" — does not fully warrant the inference that he had written all these reviews.[1] There is the same sort of uncertainty about some of the reviews reprinted from other numbers of the *Messenger* (that is, before December, 1835, and after September, 1836);[2] and also about some of the papers reprinted from *Graham's Magazine*.[3]

It has been suggested that certain of the prose articles contained in Griswold's edition were spurious,[4] — in particular, the five articles printed by Griswold in the *Literati* in place of the articles that had originally appeared in *Godey's*.[5] But, although

[1] Indeed, Professor Harrison, after assigning to Poe all the reviews published in the *Messenger* during the nine months covered by Poe's statement, excludes from his bibliography one of the items published there — that of "Mellen's Poems," — and he expresses doubt whether Poe wrote the lengthy article on Chief Justice Marshall in the *Messenger* for February, 1836 (II, 181 f.).

[2] One such item — the notice of Haxall's *Dissertation on the Diseases of the Abdomen and Thorax*, in the *Messenger* for October, 1836 (II, 725) — is singled out by Professor Harrison in a foot-note (*Poe's Works*, IX, 164).

[3] On the other hand, we can identify without much difficulty most of Poe's unsigned contributions to *Burton's Gentleman's Magazine*, with the aid of a letter of his to Burton, of June 1, 1840 (in which he specifies the number of pages written by him for each issue from July, 1839, to June, 1840), and of letters written by him to Cooke and Snodgrass (see Ingram, pp. 142–145; Woodberry, I, 212 f., 221, 242 f.; *Poe's Works*, XVII, 51 f.); and we can also identify most of his contributions to the *Broadway Journal*, through the poet's own signature appended to them in a copy of the *Journal* presented to Mrs. Whitman and now in the Huntington Library (see *Poe's Works*, I, xiii; XII, viii f.).

[4] See *Poe's Works*, I, xv; XV, ix, 263 f.; XVI, vii.

[5] See Griswold, III, 35 f., 79 f., 87 f., 101 f.; and *Poe's Works*, XV, 263 f.

Griswold was not a very conscientious editor, I can conceive of no motive for the garbling of his text or for the introduction of spurious items in the present instance. What he did, I think, was to substitute for the original *Godey* articles papers written by Poe or dressed up by him after 1846.[1] One of the suspected *Literati* articles — the paper on Mrs. Osgood [2] — appeared in the *Southern Literary Messenger* for August, 1849,[3] and is there duly accredited to Poe; and the remaining four items are all in Poe's manner.

III

The additions that will hereafter be made to the Poe canon will come mainly from the magazines for which Poe wrote; though we may expect to see still other manuscripts brought to light.[4] It is not unreasonable, for instance, to hope that the manuscript of *The Authors of America in Prose and Verse*, of which mention has been made above in the discussion of the "Lavante" pamphlet, still survives. This manuscript was probably in the hands of Griswold when he was making up his edition; in which case I suspect that it was found to track the *Literati* pretty closely, and for that reason was ignored by him. It is not

[1] Whether or not he had authority for this, it is impossible now to know.

[2] See Griswold, III, 87 f.; and *Poe's Works*, xv, 271 f.

[3] xv, 509 f.

[4] Of interest in this connection is the manuscript of a hitherto unknown poem in Poe's autograph and apparently of his composition — a valentine "To Miss Louise Olivia Hunter" — that appeared in the New York *Times* of February 14, 1932.

unlikely, too, that other manuscripts of the "Marginalia" will be discovered in the course of time. In a letter to Mrs. Richmond early in 1849,[1] Poe wrote that he had sent fifty pages of the "Marginalia" to the *Southern Literary Messenger*, five pages of it to appear in each of the next ten numbers; in reality, only five of the projected ten installments ever appeared: the manuscript for the rest may still be in existence.[2] And there are, perhaps, other tales preserved in manuscript. The assertion is made in a review of the 1845 edition of Poe's tales — inspired, so Professor Woodberry thinks,[3] by the poet — that Poe had already published "seventy-five or eighty tales," whereas but sixty-nine (exclusive of the *Pym* and the "Rodman") are known to the editors of Poe, and some of these, it is certain, were written after 1845.[4] It is, of course, very likely — to adopt another of Professor Woodberry's suggestions — that

[1] *Poe's Works*, XVII, 328 f.

[2] A small manuscript roll of "Marginalia" was among the rarities disposed of at the sale of the Stedman Library in January, 1911; and Mr. Whitty mentions (p. 233) a manuscript volume of "Marginalia" once in the possession of a Richmond printer, but now lost.

[3] II, 406.

[4] In June, 1844, Poe wrote Anthon that his tales were "in number sixty-six" (Woodberry, II, 78); and in a notice of the 1845 edition of the tales, published in the *Broadway Journal* of July 12, 1845, while he was editor, it is asserted that the tales in that edition were selected from "about seventy tales of similar length, written by Mr. Poe." On December 15, 1846, Poe wrote Eveleth (see *The Letters of Poe to Eveleth*, ed. James Southall Wilson, p. 9) that the number of his stories at that time was seventy-two.

"Mellonta Tauta," "Hop-Frog," "X-ing a Paragrab," and "Von Kempelen and His Discovery" all appear to have been written during the last two years of the poet's life.

there were included in this estimate some of Poe's miscellanies.[1] But Mr. Woodberry's discovery a few years ago of a fragment of a tale of which apparently nothing had hitherto been known, "The Lighthouse," should of itself make us hesitate to predict that there are no other tales yet to be found. Poe sent the manuscript of at least one of his tales, as we know, to friends in England, and something may perhaps be looked for from that source.[2] Mr. Ingram asserts (p. 139) that there is some reason for believing that Poe completed the "Journal of Julius Rodman," which had been abruptly brought to an end in *Burton's* for June, 1840, with his secession from the editorship of that magazine. The story may have been concluded in the *Saturday Museum*, which contained in its issue of July 22, 1842, "further extracts from the 'Narrative of a Journey to the Rocky Mountains.'"[3] And W. F. Gill in his *Life of Poe* (p. 124) speaks of an unpublished story of Poe's that remained in the hands of T. C. Clarke.

There are also reminiscences, more or less authentic, of a number of poems which have been lost but

[1] Griswold, it may be noted, included "The Philosophy of Furniture" among the tales. In the same way, Poe may have counted his essay "An Opinion on Dreams" (printed in *Burton's* for August, 1839, and first assigned to Poe by Mr. Whitty, p. lxiii) as a tale. Perhaps, too, he counted his introduction to the "Tales of the Folio Club" as a separate story (see *Poe's Works*, II, xxxvi f.).

[2] "The Spectacles" was sent to Horne in 1843 or 1844 (see *Poe's Works*, XVII, 168, and Ingram, p. 204); and before this Poe had sent to Dickens a volume of tales which he hoped to have published in England (see the *Nation* for November 24, 1910, p. 492).

[3] See the Philadelphia *United States Gazette*, July 21, 1843.

which may yet turn up in manuscript. These are:
(1) a volume of juvenilia submitted to Poe's Richmond school-teacher, Joseph H. Clarke, in 1823, and
consisting "chiefly of pieces addressed to different
little girls in Richmond who had from time to time
engaged his youthful affections"; [1] (2) a poem addressed to Master Clarke on his retirement as principal of his school in Richmond; [2] (3) "To Mary
——," [3] lines addressed to a Baltimore sweetheart [4]
and said to have been published in a Baltimore newspaper; (4) a poem in honor of Mrs. Shew and entitled
"The Beautiful Physician," [5] composed in part, so
Mrs. Shew declared, while the poet was in a delirium
following the death of his wife in 1847, and later
recast by him from jottings which Mrs. Shew had
made. [6] There is also a tradition that Poe wrote in

[1] Didier, *Life of Poe*, New York, 1879, p. 31.   [2] *Ibid.*, p. 33.

[3] These, Woodberry suggests (II, 414), were probably the same as
Poe's lines "To Mary" in the *Southern Literary Messenger* for July, 1835
(I, 636), later addressed to Mrs. Osgood under the title "To F——."
But the lines to the "Baltimore Mary" are said to have been "very
severe" and to have dealt with "fickleness and inconstancy" — a de-
scription to which Poe's lines in the *Messenger* hardly answer. Another
poem "To Mary" — and subscribed, as it happens, with the initial
"P." — appeared in the *New England Magazine* for January, 1832
(II, 72). But this, too, contains nothing of the satirical; besides, it comprises sixteen lines, while the poem said to have been published in Baltimore was only "six or eight" lines in length. And there is a brief poem,
"Lines to Mary," in the Baltimore *Saturday Visiter* of November 3, 1832;
but this poem is signed "H. T." and is evidently not Poe's.

[4] See the article of Augustus Van Cleef, *Harper's Monthly*, CXXVIII,
638 (March, 1889).

[5] Mr. Whitty suggests (p. 286) that this was perhaps a revised version
of the poem "The Great Man," found by him in manuscript in the
desk used by Poe when editor of the *Southern Literary Messenger*.

[6] See Ingram, the *Bookman*, CXXVIII, 452 f. (January, 1909).

collaboration with his friend R. M. Bird, of Philadelphia, a scenario for a play.[1]

But, as I have said, the main additions to the canon are to be sought in the magazines of Poe's time. Of two of the periodicals to which Poe contributed more or less freely, no complete files are known. These are the Baltimore *Saturday Visiter*, in which his "MS. Found in a Bottle," "A Serenade," and "The Coliseum" were first printed, and the Philadelphia *Saturday Museum*, to which he contributed divers critical articles in the early forties.[2] It is highly probable that he published in these papers other things besides those of which we have record. And there are doubtless yet other items in the periodicals and annuals of Poe's time. In particular, there are, I suspect, unidentified articles in the magazines which Poe edited — the *Southern Literary Messenger, Burton's Gentleman's Magazine, Graham's,* the *Evening Mirror,* and the *Broadway Journal.*[3] It remains, among other things, to determine just which of certain "short notices" in

---

[1] Woodberry, II, 421. Poe's statement that he had also written a poem entitled "Holy Eyes" and a novel entitled "An Artist at Home and Abroad" must, of course, be dismissed as apocryphal.

[2] See his letter to Lowell of March 27, 1843 (Woodberry, II, 21).

[3] See the *Nation* of December 23, 1909, pp. 623 f., for a list of some twenty-five brief articles published in these magazines which are probably Poe's, but which have not yet been fully authenticated. It is possible, I think, that some of the shorter poems published anonymously in the *Southern Literary Messenger* in 1834 and 1835 are Poe's; and we can be all but certain that there are other critical articles in the *Messenger* for 1845 and 1849. See also in this connection an article by Mr. T. O. Mabbott in *Notes and Queries* for December 17, 1932, p. 441.

Burton's Gentleman's Magazine attributed to **Poe** without specification of title [1] are actually Poe's and which are the work of others.[2] Mr. Whitty asserts (p. xxxvi) that Poe wrote for *Poulson's American Daily Advertiser* and for the Philadelphia *Mercury* in the early thirties; Professor Woodberry has suggested [3] that Poe probably contributed to the *Brother Jonathan* in the autumn of 1843; and in two of his letters during his final year [4] the poet refers to the *Literary World* (of which his friend E. A. Duyckinck was then editor) as though he were perhaps a contributor.[5] Mr. Whitty has told us [6] of Poe's connection with the Richmond *Examiner* in the summer of 1849, — in particular, of his republishing in its columns several of his poems; Bishop Fitzgerald is authority for the statement that Poe also contributed critical articles to the *Examiner* at this time;[7] and I have already called attention to Poe's assertions

[1] *Poe's Works*, XVI, 363 f.

[2] It is perhaps not a matter of large importance that all these scraps should be collected, but it is at least desirable that such as can be shown to be Poe's shall be definitely set down to his credit, in order that the biographer and the literary historian may avail themselves of such information as they afford. See, in this connection, an editorial in the *Atlantic Monthly*, LXXVII, 552 (April, 1896), in which it was declared that owing to the incompleteness of the editions of Poe published up to that time there remained "for the student of Poe's life and times a field of research practically unexplored."

[3] II, 424.

[4] *Poe's Works*, XVII, 361, 367.

[5] In another letter (of March 8, 1849, — *ibid.*, p. 341) he mentions having offered his tale "Von Kempelen and His Discovery" to Duyckinck for publication in the *Literary World*.

[6] *Poe's Poems*, pp. viii f., lxxvii f.

[7] See *Poe's Works*, I, 318.

that he had written for several British magazines.[1]
Hirst states in his sketch of Poe in the *Saturday
Museum* that he had also written for a "Parisian
critical journal." [2] Similarly it is asserted in Lowell's
sketch of Poe in *Graham's* that he had "contributed
several reviews" to French as well as English periodicals.[3]

Before we can feel satisfied that we have got a
complete list of Poe's writings, it will be necessary
to bring from out their hiding-places complete files
of the *Saturday Visiter* and the *Saturday Museum*;
we must also examine anew the files of the periodicals
with which Poe was connected editorially; and we
must institute a search through the remainder of the
early magazines and newspapers and annuals to
which Poe may have contributed. In particular, the
Baltimore papers of the early thirties and the Philadelphia papers of the forties must be sifted. When
this is done, it is possible that the canon of Poe's
writings will be materially enlarged.

[1] *Supra*, p. 222.   [2] Woodberry, ii, 410.   [3] *Poe's Works*, i, 382.

DATE DUE

JUN 1 6 1993	DEC 1 4 2000	
OCT 2 9 1993	APR 2 0 2001	
NOV 1 7 1993	JAN 0 6 2003	
NOV 2 7 1994		
DEC 1 4 1994	APR 1 8 2004	
APR 2 3 1995	DEC 1 3 2005	
NOV 0 7 1996		
APR 2 2 1997		
AUG 0 5 1998		
JAN 1 2 1999		
MAY 1 9 1999		
OCT 1 1 1999		